The DSDM Student Workbook

D.J. & I.J. Tudor

Galatea Training Services Ltd.

The DSDM Student Workbook

D.J. & I.J. Tudor

Published by:

Galatea Training Services Limited
St John's Vicarage
The Avenue
High Legh
Knutsford
Cheshire
WA16 6ND

Tel: +44 (0) 1706 351389
Fax: +44 (0) 1706 346031
Email: info@galatea-services.co.uk
Website: www.galatea-services.co.uk

ISBN: 0-9543071-0-0

Contents

Session 1
DSDM – Approach, Principles and Framework

1   What is RAD?

Rapid Application Development (RAD) has been used to describe everything from a well-structured "fastpath" to small systems development to the "quick and dirty" system thrown together during a lunch hour in response to a sudden commercial pressure. It should certainly be the former!

The fundamental purpose of RAD is to deliver working systems which are delivered with **high speed**, **high quality** and at **low cost**. Typically operational systems are delivered using RAD in 3-6 months.

RAD projects fundamentally and characteristically:

- use prototyping;

- use timeboxing;

- require user involvement;

- require that the team is empowered.

2   What is Prototyping?

2.1   What is prototyping within RAD?

Prototyping during development of computer systems can mean many things. It may be the development of a few screens and report formats, with no data structure behind, or it may be the first stages of construction of the working code of the system, using development tools which will generate accurate, efficient code.

Within RAD, it is intended that any prototyping will eventually become part of the working system. Initial prototypes may define the functionality in a rough, unsophisticated (but workable) way, and refinements may be added later.

The ability to deliver the eventual system from prototypes depends heavily on the sophistication of the software tools available. True RAD is only possible where sophisticated prototyping and code generating tools are not only available, but well understood by the development team. The skill of the development team in their use of the tools is a key factor in the success of prototyping.

Prototyping and workshops are complementary techniques. Prototyping will often take place within a workshop.

Evolutionary prototyping involves the delivery of the system in small but useful increments, but also ensuring a mechanism for the feedback of improvements needed, as indicated by the live use of the prototyped parts of the system.

2.2 Why prototype?

The use of prototyping, with incremental deliveries of parts of the system, means that the end-user can have the essential functions of the system quicker than if they waited for the system as a whole to be written, tested and delivered. (Of course, systems developed using RAD still need to be tested!) This means that requirements which are urgent can be addressed within a shorter timescale and business "windows of opportunity" can be met. The idea of delivering a system two years after the first needs were identified is not useful in the changing climate in which organisations have to operate.

2.3 Evolution of prototypes

Characteristically, within DSDM, prototypes undergo iterative development which facilitates an incremental evolution of the final prototype. Generally three iterations of each phase's prototyping is sufficient leading from an **initial prototype** through a **refined prototype** to a **consolidated prototype**.

Obviously iteration has to be a managed process which is not allowed to get out of hand and to this end the following are key considerations:

● **timescale** – The strict adherence to timescales ensures that prototyping cycles are not allowed to lose their focus;

● **change control** – The procedures for change control must allow change to be introduced quickly and effectively in order to enact 'RAPID';

● **configuration management** – In order to be able to backtrack to a previous prototype, strong configuration management must be enforced. Backtracking smoothly to previous dialogue designs or to adjust the course of the development must be secure with developer confidence in the current status of the development;

● **user involvement** – User involvement has to be handled sensitively to ensure that all users on the team express their ideas. 'He who shouts loudest will get served' must not be the way forward since it could result in the development being weighted in favour of serving a particular business area's requirements at the expense of other business areas.

Prototyping is used during the evolution of the new system with each new prototype adding more functionality than those produced previously.

3 Flexing Requirements

In direct contrast to the traditional approach for system development, DSDM allows the system requirements which are to be satisfied to change. In the DSDM approach, time is fixed for the life of a project, and resources are fixed as far as possible. Hence there is a need to prioritise requirements as they are elicited during the Business Study and refined during the lifecycle.

Traditionally, requirements are fixed and software is delivered which attempts to satisfy all of them, this being achieved by allowing time and resources to vary during development.

4 The 80/20 Approach

It can often be seen that, in a project, as time progresses the 'law of diminishing returns' comes into play. More time is taken to add the finishing touches and to develop those areas of the system which will be used infrequently than the time actually taken to develop the essential functionality. A fundamental assumption of the DSDM approach, therefore, is that nothing is built perfectly first time. Hence it follows that 80% of the solution can be produced in 20% of the time that it would take to produce the whole solution. Traditionally users are asked by developers to predict both current and future requirements for the new system. This, in turn, leads to requirements which are missed or anticipated but never realised and consequently systems are rarely 'future-proof'.

The premise, in DSDM, is that the business requirements will probably change anyway as understanding increases, so exhaustive work can be wasted time. Since DSDM assumes that all previous steps of the development process can be revisited as part of its iterative approach further work can be undertaken as part of the next iteration. Therefore, the current step need be completed only enough to move to the next step, since it can be finished in a later iteration.

5 Prioritisation and MoSCoW

Each of the requirements identified in the Business Area Definition is scrutinised by the development team so that the most business critical functions are developed first according to business need. Some of the non-functional requirements, such as security, may also be prioritised for early development.

The simple **MoSCoW** rules are used to achieve clear prioritisation of requirements:

Must have are requirements that are fundamental to the system. Without them the system will be unworkable and useless. These requirements are the *minimum usable subset of requirements* which the DSDM project guarantees to satisfy.

Should have are those requirements which are important but for which there is a work-around in the short term. The system will be useful and usable without them.

Could **have** represents requirements that can more easily be left out of this iteration of development and which will be set aside for future consideration if time permits.

Want **to have but won't have this time round** for those valuable requirements that can wait till later development takes place.

All of these requirements are defined as needed for the full system. The MoSCoW rules provide the basis on which decisions are made about what the project team will prioritise over the whole project and during any timebox within the project. It is essential that not everything to be achieved within a project or a timebox is mandatory for then the flexibility is lost. It is the lower level requirements that enable the teams to deliver on time by dropping out lower priority requirements when problems arise.

As new requirements arise or as existing requirements are defined in more detail, the decision must be made as to how critical they are to the success of the current work using the MoSCoW rules.

All priorities must be under review throughout the project to confirm that they are still valid.

6   Why is RAD needed?

The pressure on IT departments is to develop working computer systems for their business in a short timescale. RAD is one approach to building and maintaining computer systems which combines effective use of tools and techniques, incremental prototyping and tight project delivery timescales. The approach was first formalised by DuPont in the mid-1980s in the RIPP method (Rapid Iterative Production Prototyping). There has been increasing publicity for RAD since the publication in 1991 of James Martin's book on the subject.

RAD is aimed at the speedy delivery of business systems. This approach is usually only applicable when the project is:

- relatively small (if large, the project may be broken down into small component DSDM projects which may run in parallel);

- of limited scope and impact upon the organisation (low risk);

- does not require new or special hardware or software platform;

- able to use fourth generation (or later) tools for the rapid development of the software;

- able to be developed by practitioners highly skilled both in the use of RAD and in the development and implementation of systems in the target environment.

The key features of good RADs are:

- the use of structured techniques and prototyping;

- extensive use of CASE tools for project support, system definition and generation;

- firm project management, including some form of "time-boxing", i.e. the project is defined in terms of precise products, constrained to be completed within a pre-set maximum (and short!) time-slot;

- a sound project plan with products derived from the framework of a structured method;

- a determination to re-use existing products, (e.g. existing analysis documents as well as code and data structures) wherever feasible;

- clearly defined roles, responsibilities and levels of authority for the project personnel;

- the involvement of users through Facilitated Workshops (Joint Application Development (JAD) workshops), organised within a well-defined framework.

Facilitated workshops are used in RAD because, if used properly, they are a quicker way of discovering facts and requirements, obtaining decisions and resolving conflict than interviews or many conventional meetings. A workshop is a meeting of people involved with a project

- in specific roles;

- with specific responsibilities;

- with particular knowledge and expertise.

In comparison to the more traditional lifecycle for systems development active user involvement in RAD projects, especially in the Requirements Planning and User Design activities, is high. It is also higher, albeit at a reducing level, during construction of the system. It is this user involvement throughout which helps to compress the development time and to deliver business benefits quickly.

It has been noted that much of the functionality of a new system is developed early in the project with a disproportionate amount of time being consumed in the later stages due to re-work borne out of misunderstanding of user requirements, 'tweaking' the system and the consequent impact of such changes. RAD acts upon this observation to deliver benefits.

Naturally there are some risks associated with using RAD. These risks are many, but from the structured methods viewpoint include the possibility that products of those methods vital to the success of the project will be omitted in the interests of speed. It must be appreciated by all involved that <u>RAD is not an excuse for omitting necessary project products</u>.

Another risk involves prototyping, where the number of iterations to arrive at a satisfactory result can turn into a seemingly endless loop. Tight control of the number of prototyping iterations ('convergence toward a solution') of any particular aspect of the system must be in place. The key to this lies in the clear definition, beforehand, of the aspects to be prototyped, and the objectives of each prototyping session. The results of each session should be well-documented.

The <u>RAD approach is not an alternative to structured methods</u>. Indeed some structured methods contain details of specific fastpath frameworks for the purpose (for example Information Engineering). The increased use of prototyping is covered by some, but not all, structured methods. RAD techniques are a short-term expedient, pending the arrival of even more powerful integrated CASE (i-CASE supports analysis and design as well as producing code) tools which can handle a far greater proportion of the systems development lifecycle for us. The future impact is likely to be that the i-CASE tool support will automate much more of the physical design and construction and that RAD workshops will be used to elicit and define requirements, which will be able to be almost immediately prototyped. This will be possible, however, only when i-CASE tools are sufficiently slick in operation and friendly of face not to interfere with, and dominate, the requirements discovery session.

7 Why have Dynamic Systems Development Method (DSDM)?

Structured Methods for Systems Analysis and Design have sought to bring together the best practices for developing systems from the combined experience of Analysts and Developers. DSDM is no exception in this respect. It has evolved following the formation of the DSDM Consortium at its inaugural meeting in January 1994. At that meeting the Consortium defined itself as an independent organisation with the objective of developing and continuously evolving a public domain RAD method within a short timescale.

DSDM V1 was released early in 1995 and whilst DSDM gathered momentum, rapid evolution toward version 2 culminated in its publication late in 1995. Version 3 was launched in September 1997 and the method continues to be refined.

DSDM is a method for rapidly developing high quality systems and is perhaps more easily defined in terms of what it is not. DSDM is not a system development method which jumps straight into coding as a 'quick and dirty' unstructured alternative to good practice. It is not a licence to hack with no ancillary documentation being required.

System development can be dogged by a number of symptoms of failure, for example where the system, which is produced...

- does not meet the business requirements;

- gives poor performance;

- contains errors;

- is not accepted by users;

- is not maintainable.

All systems, bearing one or more of these hallmarks of failure, may require a lot of re-work to treat the symptom although in many cases the damage may be too great for recovery to be possible. In any case the cost will be significant both financially to the organisation and also in terms of the reputation of the IT Department and its staff within the organisation.

DSDM tackles these hallmarks of failure by addressing a number of issues advocating a holistic approach. The issues which are the focus of attention for DSDM are:

- Quality Assurance;

- Project Management;

- Estimating;

- Testing;

- User Involvement;

- Prototype Management;

- S/D lifecycle;

- Risk Assessment;

- Skills & Responsibilities;

- Change Control;

- Development Environments;

- Method Tailoring;

- Team Structures;

- Configuration Management;

- Software Procurement.

Each of these will be examined during this course, some being combined to form a session, others forming a session in their own right.

7.1   The benefits of DSDM

DSDM uses an iterative approach to system development within a prototyping environment. Users are very actively involved in the whole development process and this brings with it many benefits such as:

- the users are more likely to claim ownership for the system;

- the risk of building the wrong system is greatly reduced;

- the final system is more likely to meet the users' real business requirements;

- the users will be better trained;

- the system implementation is more likely to go smoothly.

8   The Principles of DSDM

DSDM defines NINE principles which are fundamental to the successful application of the method:

- Active user involvement is imperative;

- DSDM teams must be empowered to make decisions;

- The focus is on frequent delivery of products;

- Fitness for business purpose is the essential acceptance criterion;

- Iterative and incremental development is necessary;

- All changes during development are reversible;

- Requirements are baselined at a high level;

● Testing is integrated throughout the lifecycle;

● A collaborative and co-operative approach of all stakeholders.

8.1 Active user involvement is imperative

Whilst many methods state the importance of user involvement most do not bestow the level of responsibility upon the user which DSDM insists upon. Indeed the acceptance and delivery of this by senior management is crucial for DSDM to effectively deliver the benefits for which it is designed. Welcoming users into the development team as ACTIVE development members rather than as simply suppliers of information about business requirements is the way that this responsibility is given.

8.2 DSDM teams must be empowered to make decisions

If the DSDM team frequently has to refer to senior management for decisions regarding the functionality and other design aspects of the system, then RAPID will be compromised. By its very iterative nature, DSDM will give rise to frequent changes and some revision of the level of functionality which can be incorporated in the new system within the development time frame. The responsibility to make these decisions has to be given to the team of developers and users by management.

8.3 The focus is on frequent delivery of products

DSDM focuses on products whilst the activities required to deliver these products are the means to the end. Provided that the activity offers an engineering approach to deliver the product then this is acceptable. The flexibility in choice of activity to deliver the stated products allows the method to accommodate the tight timescales characteristic of a RAD project. Frequent delivery of those products is essential for the feedback mechanism to operate within the project thereby allowing re-assessment of the level of functionality which is possible.

8.4 Fitness for business purpose is the essential acceptance criterion

DSDM does NOT start out by rigorously defining requirements at a high level of detail, freezing these requirements and ploughing on regardless until all requirements have been met. Holding up the Requirements Specification and defensively stating that all requirements (regardless of business need) have been delivered is not what DSDM is about! Flexibility in functionality allows requirements to continuously evolve to a closer 'fitness for purpose' level at which acceptance can be achieved.

8.5 Iterative and incremental development is necessary

Whilst methods for system development are generally iterative in nature allowing backtracking, there are obstacles to this in the form of control procedures which have to be followed. It is this overhead which adds to the development time.

DSDM acknowledges the need for control but since the system is developed in incremental units with re-work openly built into the iteration change is more easily implemented. Additionally knowledge acquired in the development of earlier incremental units can be allowed to feed back into subsequent units. This assertion of an iterative and incremental development process allows the DSDM team to deliver interim aspects of the system which can then meet an immediate business requirement.

8.6 All changes during development are reversible

DSDM focuses upon an iterative approach which in turn defines the option to backtrack as necessary. The flexibility of DSDM also allows for the opportunity to 'wipe the slate clean' and reconstruct the unit rather than backtrack, the decision being based on how fundamental the change is. It should be noted however that good configuration management needs to be in place and that change will only be allowed within an incremental unit.

8.7 Requirements are baselined at a high level

DSDM baselines requirements initially at a high level allowing subsequent investigation to refine requirements and establish other baselines throughout the duration of the project.

8.8 Testing is integrated throughout the lifecycle

Testing in DSDM is woven into the method and is most certainly not 'bolted on' at the end of the development. The whole incremental unit delivery allows for testing to be carried out (and recorded) on the units by team members to test for user requirements and technical requirements. Earlier in the development, testing focuses on business requirements with the emphasis shifting toward overall functionality and system operation in the latter stages.

8.9 A collaborative and co-operative approach of all stakeholders

Whether the development of the system is internal or out-sourced, the relationship between user and developer team members has to embody all that is implied by the designation 'team', particularly a collaborative and co-operative approach. There are no winners on a failed project. Either the whole team wins or nobody does.

9 DSDM Projects and Critical Success Factors
9.1 When is DSDM more, or less, appropriate?

There are a number of factors which have to be considered before embarking on the use of DSDM for a particular project.

DSDM would require special care if the project is for:

● a real time system;

● a system where the application must have all requirements fully specified before any coding can be done;

● a safety critical system;

● the delivery of re-usable components.

Ideally a project suitable for the application of DSDM would:

● have visible functionality;

● have a clearly defined user group;

● not be computationally complex;

● if large, be divisible into smaller functional components;

● be time constrained;

● allow for prioritisation of requirements;

● have requirements which are not detailed or fixed.

9.2   Critical Success Factors for DSDM

Even if a project does not fully meet the suitability criteria as described above it may still be possible to use DSDM if certain factors which are critical for a successful project with DSDM can be assured.

The Critical Success Factors for DSDM are:

● acceptance of the DSDM philosophy by senior management and the project sponsor is of prime importance. The committment needs to be maintained throughout the project and it must be realised that not everything may be delivered by the team but that what is delivered, will be delivered on time!;

● management must authorise the team to make decisions – there is no time for a DSDM team to wait for decisions to be made by senior management who may find that they cause delay by having to assimilate the full facts on which to base their decision. DSDM teams must be given authority to make decisions and make them quickly;

● end-user involvement must be wholeheartedly committed both by the users and the senior management of the organisation;

● incremental delivery must be acceptable to the organisation;

- easy access to other team members – communication between end users and developers must be easy possibly including dedicated office space where DSDM progress is not impeded by the telephone and other interruptions;

- whenever individuals change their job there is an inevitable settling-in period before the person becomes effective. For this reason a stable DSDM team is crucial to avoid the inevitable delays that new team members would incur whilst they 'get up to speed';

- team highly skilled – there is no time within a DSDM project for team members to climb the learning curve of techniques and tools. For this reason a balanced team which is comprised of highly skilled complementary individuals is most effective;

- size of the team – a small team will reduce the overhead for communication but should be large enough to encourage ownership of the new system;

- a supportive and co-operative relationship must exist between developers and users such that management overheads on the project should not impose an unreasonable burden. A flexible attitude should allow change to take place within the iterative style of DSDM. It is essential that system requirements should evolve without unnecessary change management control procedures, for example;

- development technology – should be in place both technically and with the necessary operational skills for the environment being vested in the team.

10   DSDM Development Process Framework

DSDM is defined within its Process Framework to be a lifecycle approach which is put forward to be tailored to suit individual projects. The default lifecycle ("three pizzas and a cheese") is entirely consistent with frequent product delivery, iterative and incremental development, active user involvement, interwoven testing and the reversal of all changes.

10.1   Lifecycle overview

There are FIVE phases in the DSDM lifecycle:

- Feasibility Study;

- Business Study;

- Functional Model Iteration;

- Design and Build Iteration;

● Implementation
(with opportunities to move back to previous phases being possible)

10.2 Feasibility Study

Over a period of a few weeks the feasibility study seeks to confirm the project suitability for DSDM and if it is not may result in the project moving across to a more traditional structured method approach. Various options for the technical solution will be considered and timescales and costings will be estimated. The Feasibility Report will then detail the system scope, the problem which the system must address as well as the chosen technical and business options to 'run with'.

10.3 Business Study

Once the Feasibility Study has been agreed the Business Study phase can be initiated to scope business functions to be included in the new system, to identify the types of user who need to be drafted into the team, to classify functions according to importance (essential, nice to have or whatever), to confirm that DSDM is still appropriate and finally to provide the foundation for development. An important aspect to Business Study is the development of a prototyping plan defining who will be involved and what types of prototype will be developed.

10.4 Functional Model Iteration

The definition of the system from Business Study has now been agreed and Senior Management committed to proceed. Prototypes are developed as a means of teasing out functional requirements detail which can be demonstrated to user representatives for iterative enhancement. It is also necessary to establish non-functional requirements such as performance level, security issues, networking facilities and access rights etc. With the increased level of detail about system functionality an implementation strategy with accompanying cost/benefit and risk analyses can be fleshed out.

10.5 Design and Build Iteration

The working prototypes from Functional Model Iteration are modified to satisfy the non-functional requirements for the new system which have been agreed at the end of the previous phase. This phase produces a tested system which satisfies all functional and non functional requirements, accompanied by the documentation of performance of the design prototypes which are produced.

10.6 Implementation

The tested system from the design and build iteration is then set up in the user environment so that users can be trained in its use as well as to get their views on its future development to be included in the project review document. As part of the implementation procedure a user manual is produced in much the same way as implementation proceeds in a traditional method.

10.7 Prototyping cycles

Functional Model and Design and Build Iterations each consist of four stages which make up a prototyping cycle:

- identify;

- agree;

- create;

- review.

10.7.1 Identify prototypes

By prioritising the functional and non-functional requirements those which are essential to be prototyped can be identified whilst those which are 'nice to have' can be deferred for the time being. The prototyping activities will thus be focused. In this way the application is divided into possible prototypes in line with what are the system critical areas offering greatest business benefit to specific business areas.

The focus is also maintained by defining the acceptance criteria before development ensues and also to focus on testing activities from the outset.

10.7.2 Agree schedule

As stated before a DSDM project is time-constrained and therefore it is important to control the time spent on each prototype, focusing on the essential. If time permits it may be possible to include some of the 'nice to haves' but this would depend on how many additional requirements are spawned by the prototyping activities.

The time frame for the development in a DSDM will NOT be allowed to 'slip' and users must appreciate that if they require additional areas to be investigated or additional functions to be incorporated then choices will have to be made about what will have to be left out to accommodate this.

10.7.3 Create prototype

A prototype can be performed on paper or at the terminal and, in the early phases of DSDM, will involve users and developers as they explore the business requirements. Later as the emphasis shifts to performance and other non-functional requirements the bulk of the effort will be developer time.

10.7.4 Review prototype

After development prototypes have to be reviewed culminating in the Prototyping Review Document which will identify:

- which objectives have been met;

- which areas have been 'forced out' for later development to achieve the project's timescale;

- the acceptability of the basic functionality.

The review also serves to confirm that the project is on-track as well as getting users to increase their ownership at every opportunity both in terms of what has been developed as well as the future direction. This escalating feeling of ownership ('incremental ownership') will make a significant contribution to the acceptance of the system when completed.

11 The Prototyping Approach of DSDM

Prototype demonstration with user members of the team opens the user mindset to the possibilities which there are for the new system. Provided this ambition is in a controlled context, these ideas should not get out of hand and the final product will be innovative for the business. Development moves on apace since the user is able to see and participate early and have an immediate input to the shape of the new system.

DSDM prototypes pass through a number of iterations (three on average) to the final version. Earlier versions have not completed development and therefore if implemented they would almost certainly cause problems. A DSDM project is carried out in a tight timeframe and consequently prototypes are not built to throw away. They should be built to a high standard consistent with incremental evolution to the final system.

11.1 Categories of prototype

A prototype usually serves a number of purposes which DSDM associates with four types of prototype. Their definition is consistent with clarification of their purpose:

- **business prototype**: the purpose here is to demonstrate the business functions being automated;

- **usability prototype**: used to investigate aspects of the user interface which do not affect functionality;

- **performance and capacity prototype**: to ensure that the system will be able to handle the workload successfully;

- **capability/technique prototype**: to test out a particular design approach.

11.1.1   Business prototype

A business prototype is employed by developers to confirm to the users that they understand the functional requirements which the users wish the system to have. It affords the users the opportunity to correct misunderstanding and enhance the developers' understanding. By its use early in the project, feedback from users will enable the evolutionary development of the system to incorporate enhancements to the functionality and also to the non-functional requirements.

Before the prototyping session the users must be briefed so that they understand the purpose of the session. They should be told that the prototype is not designed to look good, nor is it going to check for errors on data entry etc.

The initial business prototype session is run early so that the 'course of the ship' is largely correct from the outset. This initial session may well be run at the end of the feasibilty study and will be based on high level understanding which will provoke the outpouring of ideas from the users. It is the foundation on which the system will be **built right**.

11.1.2   Usability prototype

The focus in usability is upon how easy and intuitive the users find the operation of the system to be. There is only one way to test this, and that is to allow the users to work with the system and assess their reactions to it. Essentially a usability prototype is a mock up of the system where the user can perhaps enter some samples of real data and find out how to navigate the system without the system doing any of the background functional processing. It should be noted that the developer must be careful not to present a front-end which gives unrealistic expectations which can not be supported by the background processing activities which it is possible to develop.

It is important to arrive at a usable design since the users will then quickly pick up how to operate the system and the training overhead will be reduced.

A style guide, if present, is useful for ensuring that the interface is consistent with other systems to which users have been exposed and have experience, assuming that the usability of the style has been previously assessed and found acceptable. A high level usability prototype is built in the Functional Model Iteration to elicit a basic workable user interface. Later on in the Design and Build Iteration the interface is refined.

11.1.3   Performance and capacity prototype

The performance & capacity prototype is used primarily by developer team members to confirm that the system will cope with the volume of work and peak loading levels for it. It is used to test that performance will be acceptable for all types of functionality which will be expected of it. Test scenarios are set up to establish system performance whilst changing certain aspects of the system. System bottlenecks are identified and graphs of performance versus workload are produced to illustrate the circumstances under which the system may slow. Automation, if available, can be most useful in performance testing.

Existing business prototypes can be used for testing performance and to confirm that certain levels of functionality can be not only provided but provided in a way which gives acceptable performance in the systems operating environment.

11.1.4   Capability/technique prototype

There are usually a number of technical options from which a chosen option can be selected. These options include how to build the system and which tools to use. Developers will use capability/technique prototypes to try out design approaches and tools to help make the choice by assessing the PROs and CONs of each. The tool set available within the organisation are usually already in place but the tools still need to be assessed for appropriateness to the DSDM project. This should be done early during Feasibility Study to select the most technically appropriate way forward. Later during Design & Build the options of which approach to take can be assessed using a design capability/technique prototype.

12   The Prototyping Session

The prototyping session, like any other meeting must have clearly-defined objectives, deliverables and an agenda. For the session to work a number of inputs to the process may be needed:

- Prototype scope;

- Requirements catalogue/business objective;

- Entity model;

- Data dictionary;

- Function hierarchies + DFDs;

- User roles;

- Installation standards.

The agenda will need to cover at least the following topics:

- **Introduction to the prototyping session, and scope**: this will clearly state the objectives, and limit the possibility of unproductive sessions;

- **Education of attendees**: this will usually include the end-users for, and with, whom the system is being designed, may be necessary. They may not have been party to earlier workshops or prototyping sessions and may need to be brought up to date on progress. It may also be useful to set the prototyping session in the context of other planned sessions before and after the current one;

● **Demonstration**: a demonstration of the design thus far if appropriate, or of changes made from a previous session with the same end users may be necessary;

● **Summary of actions**: the actions to be taken within the session need to be defined. These need to be reviewed at the end of the session.

Documentation needs to be kept of the changes made during the prototyping session. This may not need to be a laborious listing of actions, the prototyping tool may provide details of changes from a previous version. Either way it is possible to classify the required changes as:

● Cosmetic;

● Local (this screen only);

● Global (affects several screens);

● Fundamental (very wide area of effects).

Before any prototyping begins, it must be ensured that the previous version of the system is **baselined** and could be returned to exactly as it was, should the prototyping session fail for some reason. With DSDM, because of incremental development and delivery, the previous version could be the live version of the system, already in use by the end-user.

13   Risks of Prototyping

Some of the main risks to the prototyping approach are:

● **Insufficient analysis and design**: design and construction may be undertaken without a good definition of the underlying data structures and functions. This will lead to inflexibility and difficulty of maintenance. Inappropriate grouping of functions and data can also make maintenance difficult, since aspects which are related may not all be handled together. Any change may thus have a wider impact on the system and it may be hard to identify the range of effect of changes;

● **Final product**: users may try to overdesign. DSDM is concerned with delivering raw functionality first and adding refinements later. However, the user may try to achieve the "perfect" system first time;

● **The prototyping tool may have too few facilities**: it may not be possible to easily and quickly translate the user's requirements into a working prototype;

- **Iteration may continue for too long**: this must be actively controlled by limiting the number of sessions to a pre-set number. See management of prototyping below;

- **Documentation may not be kept up to date/consistent**: it is difficult to document and construct at the same time. If the tool provides insufficient help in this area, it may be wise to have a person present for the session with the role of documenting what is changed.

14 Benefits of Prototyping

Expert personnel, supported by the appropriate tools, can achieve Rapid Application Development. The prototyping session also:

- enables rapid development;

- is an effective method of communication;

- can give greater accuracy in addressing user requirements;

- increases user involvement, making it easier to see problems and possibilities;

- obtains commitment from the end-users, who build the system;

- instils confidence, since progress can be seen.

15 Management of Prototyping

If timeboxes are to be strictly adhered to, then prototyping cycles must not be allowed to run out of control losing sight of the primary focus of delivering priority business functions. In general around three iterations of the prototyping cycle are appropriate for DSDM taking the prototype through the three stages of an initial **investigative** prototype, a **refining** prototype and finally a **consolidating** prototype.

As mentioned previously, prototypes are configuration items and it must be possible to backtrack to previous versions if the functionality is seen to be diverging from the primary focus. As configuration items, there will therefore be three prototypes created on the road to an acceptable functional model (FMI) and three on the road to the delivered system (DBI).

Of course all team members must be confident of which version is the current version and procedures/tool support must be in place to manage this.

15.1 Successful prototyping

In order to deliver a successful outcome there are a number of factors which need to be implemented:

- **Commitment of senior management**: prototyping requires a very high level of user involvement than traditional methods and therefore senior management must appreciate this and commit to making their staff available. It is the Project Manager who must negotiate to sort out any problems this may cause;

- **Collaboration and consensus**: the developers and users must collaborate throughout the DSDM project especially during prototyping;

- **What to prototype**: the Outline Prototyping plan which is produced by the Project Manager will detail which of the four categories of prototype are appropriate for particular areas of the project;

- **Horizontal vs. vertical approach**: the choice here is whether to divide the application in a horizontal or vertical way. A **horizontal approach** means that the whole system is built at a high level first. The advantage of this is that it will create a better understanding of the concept of the whole system where this is poorly understood. The **vertical approach** means that a section of the system is developed through its increments until it is fully understood when the focus moves to work on the next section of the system. The advantage here is that it allows incremental delivery of parts of the system for immediate business benefit;

- **Where to focus effort**: prototype development should concentrate on functionality and usability rather than on design;

- **Testing prototypes**: testing should be integrated throughout, the testing being carried out by the user-developer team on the incremental products;

- **Configuration management**: excellent configuration management is essential in a prototyping environment and the project manager should ensure that good configuration management practices are in place and understood by the team;

- **Support infrastructure and prototyping tools**: the teams must have the right tools at the right time. Success in the DSDM approach requires the infrastructure and tools to support prototyping.

Notes

DSDM

Dynamic Systems
Development Method

Approach, Principles and
Framework

© TCC   DSDMP/1/ 1

Session Objectives

• What is RAD/DSDM?

• Why is RAD needed?

• Why have DSDM?

• The Principles of DSDM

• The Process
  The Framework
  The Life Cycle
  When to Use DSDM

• Prototyping

© TCC   DSDMP/1/ 2

DSDM

A Rapid Application Development Method which does
not sacrifice quality and brings together best practices
for RAD from the combined experience of DSDM
Consortium members.

• "de facto" standard for RAD, worldwide

• vendor-independent

• Consortium members "blue-chip" companies

• evolving/refining:
  Version 1   1995
  Version 2   1996
  Version 3   1997

© TCC   DSDMP/1/ 3

Notes

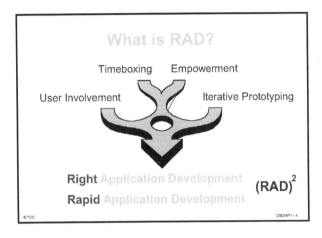

What is RAD?

Timeboxing   Empowerment

User Involvement   Iterative Prototyping

Right Application Development $(RAD)^2$

Rapid Application Development

© TCC   DSDMP1/ 4

What is prototyping?

- Evolutionary prototyping is the means of developing the new system

- Transaction-based prototypes are developed in a planned iterative process

- More functionality is added with each completed prototype

© TCC   DSDMP1/ 5

Prototyping iterations

investigate   refine   consolidate

Timebox

© TCC   DSDMP1/ 6

Notes

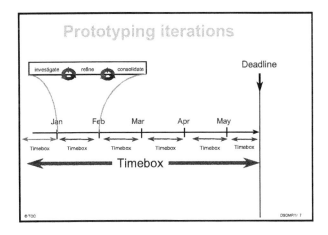

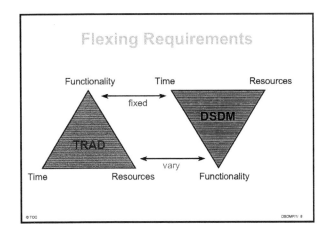

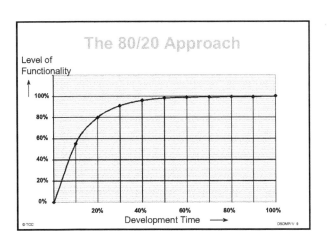

Notes

Prioritisation

Must have
o
Should have
Could have
o
Would like but Won't have

© TCC   DSDMP1/ 10

DSDM

IS:
A Rapid Application Development Method which does not sacrifice quality and brings together best practices for RAD from the combined experience of DSDM Consortium members

IS NOT:
Straight into code
Quick & Dirty
Unstructured
Alternative to good practice
Licence to 'Hack'
Indisciplined approach
Documentation-free zone

© TCC   DSDMP1/ 11

DSDM

**Tackles major reasons for
system development failures**

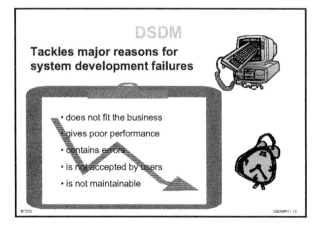

• does not fit the business
• gives poor performance
• contains errors
• is not accepted by users
• is not maintainable

© TCC   DSDMP1/ 12

Notes

The Benefits of DSDM

- user ownership of the system is more likely

- reduced risk of building the wrong system

- the final system is more likely to meet the users' real business requirements

- users will be better trained

- system implementation is more likely to go smoothly

© TCC DSDMP/1/ 13

Key Components for DSDM

DSDM

People
Tools
Management
Method

© TCC DSDMP/1/ 14

What issues does DSDM address?

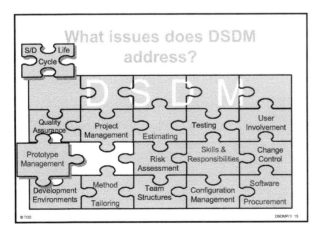

S/D Life Cycle

DSDM

Quality Assurance — Project Management — Estimating — Testing — User Involvement

Prototype Management — Risk Assessment — Skills & Responsibilities — Change Control

Development Environments — Method Tailoring — Team Structures — Configuration Management — Software Procurement

© TCC DSDMP/1/ 15

Notes

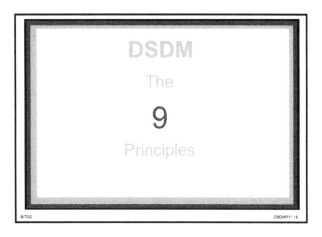

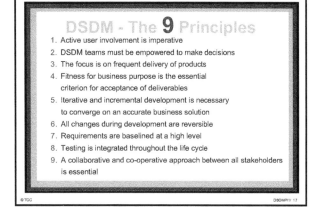

Notes

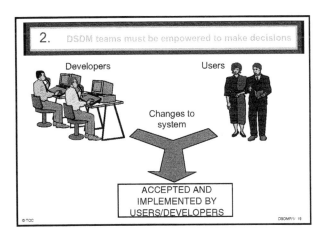

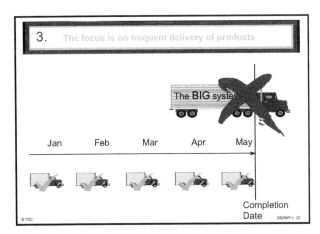

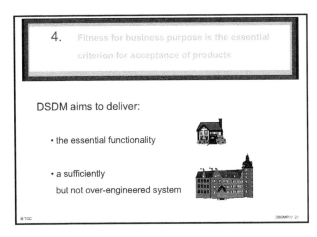

Notes

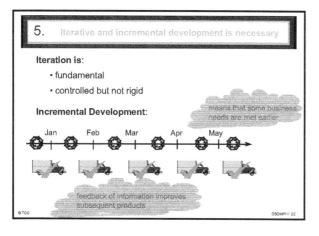

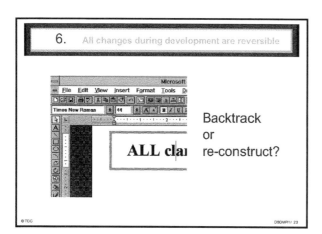

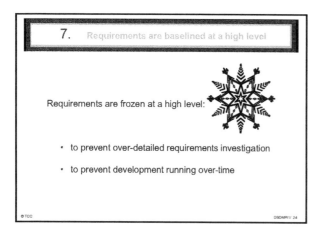

Notes

8. Testing is integrated throughout the life cycle

Testing is integrated throughout the entire life cycle:

Incremental products are tested and reviewed,
as they are delivered, by users and developers

• to ensure requirements are satisfied

• to ensure technical requirements are being met

9. A collaborative and co-operative approach
of all stakeholders is essential

• low level requirements NOT fixed at outset

• approach must be flexible

• responses to change must be rapid
(change control must not interfere with progress)

DSDM

When is it and when is it not the
appropriate method to use?

Notes

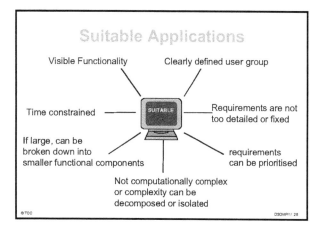

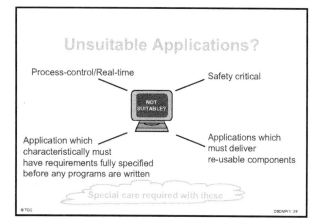

Notes

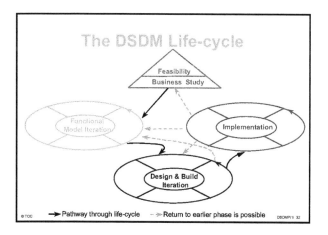

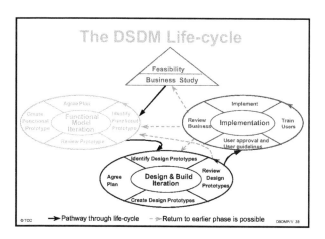

Notes

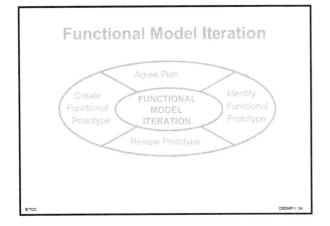

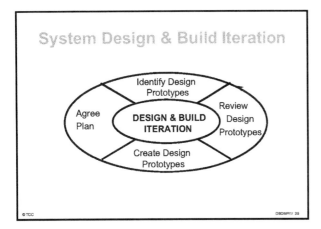

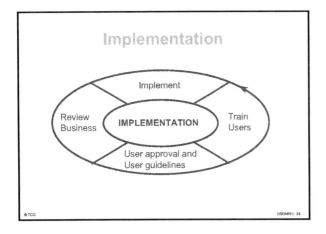

Notes

DSDM Phases

Each phase defined in terms of:

- **objectives** of the phase

- business and IT **roles** involved

- **preconditions** for entry

- **products** to be delivered

© TCC   DSDMP/1/ 37

Feasibility

Objectives

- Can we meet business requirement?
- Suitable for DSDM?
- Possible technical solutions
- "First-cut" cost/time estimates

Preconditions

- Agreement of Scope
- Agreed definition of business problem

Roles

- Business analysts
- Proposed users
- Tech. specialists
- Senior user management

Products

- Feasibility Report
- Feasibility Prototype (opt.)
- Outline Plan

© TCC   DSDMP/1/ 38

Business Study

Objectives

- Scope the business processes
- Define prototypes
- Identify user representatives
- Prioritise requirements
- Reassess if DSDM suitable
- Firm basis for technical development
- Scope non-functional requirements

Preconditions

- Agreement of Feasibility Report (both development and DSDM use)

Roles

- Business analysts
- Proposed users
- Senior user management
- System architect

Products

- Business Area Definition (BAD)
- Systems Architecture Definition (SAD)
- Prioritised Requirements List
- Outline Prototyping Plan

© TCC   DSDMP/1/ 39

Notes

Functional Model Iteration

Objectives
- Demonstrate required functionality (working and static models)
- Record non-functional Requirements

Preconditions
- Agreement of BAD and OPP
- Prototying environment in place
- Commitment of end-user time

Roles
- Business analysts
- Proposed users
- Senior user management
- Designer/programmers

Products
- Functional Model
- Functional Prototypes
- Non-functional Requirements List
- Functional Model Review Records
- Implementation Strategy
- Development Risk Analysis Report

© TCC   DSDMP/1/ 40

System Design & Build Iteration

Objectives
- Refine Functional Prototypes to meet non-functional requirements
- Engineer application to demonstrably satisfy user requirements

Preconditions
- Agreed Functional Prototypes
- Agreed non-functional requirements
- Agreed findings/changes of scope
- Design and build environment in place

Roles
- Business analysts
- Designer/programmers
- Proposed users
- Senior user management

Products
- Design Prototypes
- Design Prototype Review Records
- Tested System
- Test Records

© TCC   DSDMP/1/ 41

Implementation

Objectives
- Place tested system in user environment
- Train users
- Determine future requirements
- Train operators and support staff

Preconditions
- Agreement of Tested system
- Training time available for users
- Target environment in place

Roles
- Business analysts
- Proposed end-users
- Trainers
- Technical Authors
- Operations and support staff
- Senior user management

Products
- User Documentation
- Trained User Population
- Delivered System
- Project Review Document

© TCC   DSDMP/1/ 42

Notes

The Prototyping Approach of DSDM

DSDM Prototypes undergo:

* iterative development
* incremental evolution to the final system

DSDM Prototype Categories:

* business
* usability
* performance/capacity
* capability/technique

© TCC DSDMP/U 43

Business Prototype

Business:

* focuses on functionality
* developer demonstrates functional business requirements
* demonstrates the developer's understanding of user requirements
* confirms 'building the right system'

© TCC DSDMP/U 44

Usability Prototype

Usability:

* focuses on user interface
* illustrates system ease of use
* user tests ease of use of the system

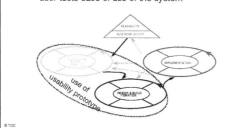

© TCC DSDMP/U 45

Notes

Performance & Capacity Prototype

Performance & Capacity:
- focuses on non-functional aspects
- developer tests that the system meets performance requirements

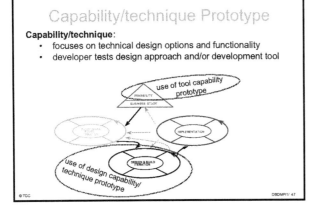

© TCC   DSDMP1/ 46

Capability/technique Prototype

Capability/technique:
- focuses on technical design options and functionality
- developer tests design approach and/or development tool

© TCC   DSDMP1/ 47

Vertical & Horizontal Prototypes

Functions

1	2	3	4	5	6	7	8	9			

depth of development

© TCC   DSDMP1/ 48

Notes

Risks of Prototyping

- Insufficient analysis and design

- "Final" product - users may try to "over-engineer"

- Prototyping tool - may have too few facilities

- Iteration - must be closely controlled

- Documentation - must be kept up-to-date/consistent

© TOC   DSDMP/1/ 49

Benefits of Prototyping

- Rapid development

- Effective method of communication - greater accuracy addressing user requirements

- Increased user involvement - easier to see problems and possibilities

- Commitment - users "build" the system

- Confidence - progress can be seen

© TOC   DSDMP/1/ 50

What issues does DSDM address?

D S D M

Quality Assurance	Project Management	Estimating	Testing	User Involvement
Prototype Management	S/D Life Cycle	Risk Assessment	Skills & Responsibilities	Change Control
Development Environments	Method Tailoring	Team Structures	Configuration Management	Software Procurement

© TOC   DSDMP/1/ 51

Session 2
DSDM – People Issues

1. Introduction

One of the major factors for the success of a DSDM project is the people who are involved. It is therefore imperative that the DSDM team is organised in a sensitive and effective way. This session covers the major people issues which affect the outcome of a DSDM project:

- the Team Structure;

- the Roles and Responsibilities;

- the Empowerment of the Team;

- the Essential Skills of the Team.

The underlying philosophy of DSDM which the team has to service is to:

'....deliver a usable system on time'

But what is meant by a **'usable system'** and how is the delivery to be achieved **'on time'**?

1.1 The "people aspects" of building a usable system

A usable system is a lot more than a technically correct system which is error free. It must support business activities in the correct way and not hinder user activity.

'Build the system right' and also 'Build the right system'

To build the right system DSDM uses an iterative prototyping approach which prioritises requirements for maximum benefit and allows the specification of the system to evolve as development proceeds. Building the right system also requires that the communication problems between users and IT staff which have plagued many a project in the past are eliminated. DSDM achieves this by making users part of the system development team where their involvement is truly active. Their on-going commitment on a regular basis gives them a sense of ownership because they are able to influence the development as it progresses. This partnership between users and developers must operate in a 'no blame' atmosphere which is non-threatening to individual members (users or developers) of the team otherwise members may well be inhibited and the project starved of total input.

1.2   On time

If the team is to deliver the system on time there must be no decision bottlenecks. For this reason the team must be empowered to agree changes in functionality without recourse to senior management and to carry through those decisions without any fear of comeback. The policy of presenting frequent deliverables which are developed in a tight timescale (timebox), although it puts the team under pressure, has the psychological effect of making progress visible. This boost spurs the team on to the next stage of development.

2.   DSDM Teams

In a traditional system development the signed-off user specification is used in a defensive way by developers to point out that "it isn't in the spec and therefore we didn't agree to do that". Either users don't get the functionality or extra has to be paid for it to be introduced. Either way the relationship between users and developers is damaged with blame being cast.

The no-blame anti-fault policy of DSDM tackles this through equal joint responsibility and development. It is essential that individual responsibility is understood and accepted, but that if problems do develop, it is seen as a team failure rather than an individual's. The team should then continue to work together to resolve the difficulty.

DSDM teams have a number of roles defined some of which must be assigned to user team members, some which must be assigned to developer team members and some which could be assigned to either user or developer. It should be noted however that any one individual may be assigned to more than one role.

Composition of the team depends on both personalities and practicalities although the team size is likely to be between two and six. Where a project is large, of course, it can be split into a number of development teams. The project manager gives consideration to what mix of team will be effective but should always be prepared to change the structure later if it is not working. This is assuming that breaking up relationships which have developed does not endanger the progress of future work.

3   DSDM Roles and Skills

The roles which are defined for assignment in DSDM are shown below. The designations (U) and (D) are intended to indicate those roles which are typically User (U) or IT/Developer (D) roles:

- Executive Sponsor (U);

- Visionary (U);

- Ambassador User (U);

- Advisor User (U);

- Project Manager (U/D);

- Technical Co-ordinator (D);

- Team Leader (D);

- Developer/Senior Developer (D);

- Facilitator(U/D);

- Scribe (U/D);

- Other Specialist Roles.

3.1   Executive Sponsor (U)

The Executive Sponsor is the 'DSDM Champion' who is committed to the method and wants the system. The Executive Sponsor is the owner of the system, has responsibility for it and must hold a sufficiently high position in the organisation to be able to resolve business issues and make financial decisions. This role has a crucial responsibility to ensure and enable fast progress throughout the project, cutting through the bureaucracy and politics that impede development.

Specific Skills:

- authority to commit funds and resources;

- ability to question and be decisive;

- politically aware with good knowledge of the business.

Responsibilities:

- the 'owner' of the system with ultimate responsibility for it;

- to make effective and rapid decisions;

- risk assessment and any corrective action;

- ensure funds and resources are available as needed;

- ensure business justification continues to be valid;

- to be committed and available throughout the project.

3.2 Visionary (U)

The Visionary is a user role with responsibility for getting a project started through a committed and enthusiastic approach to the project and its business goals. The Visionary should remain involved throughout the design and delivery process to ensure the original objectives are being met. If any issues arise during the project which must be considered by higher management, the visionary will either provide the decision or provide higher management with the business viewpoint upon which the decision can be made.

Specific Skills:

- excellent communicator;

- extremely business aware;

- very aware of technical options.

Responsibilities:

- promote translation of vision into working practice;

- take a wide view;

- contribute to key requirement, design and review sessions;

- resolve conflicts across business areas owned by the visionary;

- ensure availability of user resources;

- monitor progress <u>in line with original vision</u>;

- must be committed and available throughout.

3.3 Ambassador User (U)

The Ambassador User generally comes from the business area being addressed and becomes an integral part of the development team. Working closely with the Team Leader and Technical Co-ordinator, the Ambassador User provides the key focus for design decisions driving the system design forward. Additionally the role is responsible for bringing other users' inputs and ideas to the various sessions. The holder of the Ambassador User role must have the desire, authority, responsibility and knowledge to be able to ensure that the **right system is built** for the business. This does not necessarily imply a senior position within the organisation, but a level of empowerment during the project to fulfil the role and an allocation of time to fully participate in the project as required.

Specific Skills:

- good knowledge of the business area and politics;

- high level view of how the system must function;

- good communicator, able to pass on knowledge and ideas.

Responsibilities:

- to champion user input to requirement and design sessions;

- to provide detail of business scenarios;

- to gather user opinions and secure agreement;

- to provide input to prototyping;

- review documentation, review and accept delivered software;

- to provide user documentation and manage user training;

- to organise and control user testing.

3.4 Advisor User (U)

The Advisor User brings day-to-day knowledge of the job being automated and ultimately will be one of the users of the new system.

Specific Skills:

- practical knowledge of the business area;

- able to communicate knowledge and ideas.

Responsibilities:

- provide information on request;

- practical considerations to be input to prototyping and review;

- to approve design and prototypes for practical use;

- to participate in functional and usability testing.

3.5 Project Manager (U/D)

The Project Manager is not part of the individual development teams but has overall responsibility for ensuring that the product is delivered, together with responsibilities for co-ordination and reporting to management.

Specific Skills:

- good communicator;

- plan and manage project;

- politically aware;

- business aware;

- ability to solve technical and personnel problems.

Responsibilities:

- report to management/steering committee;

- plan and schedule project;

- monitor progress;

- manage risk;

- teams motivation;

- set team objectives;

- chair project meetings;

- manage user involvement;

- exception handling;

- identify specialist roles and resource them;

- handle project team problems.

The Project Manager is chosen by the team on the basis of his/her understanding of both business and technical issues as well as the ability to relate well to users. The Project Manager must facilitate decisions by the team if necessary (arbitrate not dictate) and must appreciate the pressure which DSDM teams are under to avoid 'burnout' of team members.

3.6 Technical Co-ordinator (D)

The Technical Co-ordinator is involved on a part-time basis in all individual development teams reporting to the Project Manager. The role ensures that teams work in a consistent way, and that the project is technically coherent and sound overall. The role can incorporate that of Database Administrator (DBA) or provide the interface with the DBA during the development process. The role provides the "glue" that holds the project together while advising on technical decisions and innovation.

Specific Skills:

- experience of tools;

- experience of standards;

- senior technician who has seen the problems before;

- good technical vision.

Responsibilities:

- determine the technical environment;

- control configuration management procedures;

- ensure adherence to standards;

- advise on and co-ordinate each team's technical activities;

- attend prototyping sessions to advise standards;

- ensure the maintainability objectives are met;

- agree and control the software architecture;

- identify opportunities for reuse;

- manage release control.

3.7 Team Leader (D)

The Team Leader ensures that the team functions as a whole, and meets its objectives.

Specific Skills:

- good communicator/listener;

- technically competent;

- good understanding of business;

- analytical;

- fully trained in RAD techniques (Facilitated Workshops, prototyping).

Responsibilities:

- maintain the focus on Business Area Definition;

- make sure that user requirements are addressed;

- set up user/developer prototyping sessions;

- create an environment for full participation of team members;

- steer prototyping sessions to achieve objectives on time;

- change control and documentation;

- promote good team morale and motivation.

3.8 Developer/Senior Developer (D)

A Senior Developer models and interprets user requirements, and converts them into prototypes and deliverable code, using the Business Study document and further user feedback. The role also documents and develops any non-prototypable elements of the system. A Developer assists with these tasks as part of DSDM skills development.

Specific Skills (Senior Developer):

- experience of prototyping techniques;

- experience of tools and other techniques being used;

- good listener/communicator;

- good business area awareness.

Specific Skills (Developer):

- knowledge of prototyping techniques;

- knowledge of tools and other techniques being used;

- good listener/communicator;

- business awareness.

Responsibilities:

- create detailed documentation as necessary;

- work with users to define business requirements, create prototypes and finished programs;

- create other components, such as a logical data model;

- create technical test scripts;

● review/test personal work and that of others.

3.9 Facilitator (U/D)

The Facilitator is independent of the project team. The facilitator is responsible for managing the workshop process and is the catalyst for preparation and communication. The Facilitator is responsible for the context and not the content of the workshop.

Specific Skills:

● excellent inter-personal skills;

● excellent communicator;

● good presentation skills;

● ability to be impartial;

● competent in the workshop process;

● business awareness.

Responsibilities:

This facilitator role brings with it the specific responsibilities of:

● agreeing the scope of the workshop with the Project Manager;

● planning the workshop;

● familiarisation with the business area;

● interviewing participants to ensure their suitability and that any pre-work is complete;

● facilitating the workshop to meet its objectives;

● reviewing the workshop against its objectives.

3.10 Scribe (U/D)

The Scribe sits in on team meetings, facilitated workshops and prototyping sessions to record requirements, agreements and decisions reached. These are then either read back and agreed by the team at the time or circulated for review or agreement. At these sessions many issues are raised and comments made, which either affect the area being discussed or prototyped but cannot be immediately dealt with. These are also documented.

Specific Skills:

- good communicator/listener;

- technically and business aware;

- good written communicator.

Responsibilities:

- record all points/actions relevant to the system;

- assist in interpretation of such documentation;

- project documentation distribution.

3.11 Other Specialist Roles

Specialists brought in as required:

Business Consultant

An expert in a particular field to offer advice and guidance or to produce a document.

Business Modeller

To provide modelling expertise in a particular technique e.g. OO or structured modelling.

Business Architect

To undertake business planning, advise on business structure and flow, and undertake impact analysis/review on the overall business model.

Business Process Co-ordinator

To promote, develop and co-ordinate the new or changed business processes.

Technical Consultants

To provide expertise in specific areas such as networks, database design, operational considerations, tools usage, technical reviews.

Human Factors Specialist

To advise on the design of the user interface for maximum productivity, comfort, usability, etc.

Capacity/Performance Planner

To advise on capacity requirements for final computer system; to advise on any performance requirements.

Re-use Assessor

To advise on any suitable reusable components from the existing library which could be used in this development. At the end of the project, to consider any components which could be put into the reusable library.

Security Specialist

To advise on any security requirements.

Data Architect

To advise on common data standards, provide impact analysis on other systems via the use of common data and review the data model.

Configuration Manager

If the organisation has identified configuration management as a necessary independent function: however there should also be a configuration librarian role within the team.

Quality Manager

As required by the organisation's quality management system.

Systems Integrator

Depending on the size of the total project, there may be a need for a Systems Integrator to take responsibility for the final assembly of the project components. This is normally either an individual re-deployed from one of the DSDM teams or the Technical Co-ordinator.

Support and Maintenance Team Representatives

If the support is not to be done by developers, the support team needs to be involved in the development in order to gain knowledge to enable them to successfully provide support to the end users.

Operations Co-ordinator.

The computer system must be acceptable to the operations department. Therefore it is necessary to involve the people who will be responsible for the operational aspects, both during design and implementation. Also to ensure that the new system is included in the Disaster Recovery Plan for the site as relevant.

Infrastructure Provider

To provide and set up the hardware, system software and comms environment required for both development and production.

Service/Help Desk Manager

To advise and negotiate the Service Level Agreement for the final computer system if required. To agree how the system will be handled by the Help Desk if relevant.

Testing Manager

To produce the testing strategy, to ensure the correct set-up of the test environment and to co-ordinate testing activity.

Metrics Manager

To assist with estimating and Function Point counting for the project. To collect and analyse metrics once the project is complete to feedback into the estimating process.

Compliance Specialist

To advise on legal, data protection, audit trail, Year 2000 and any other compliance aspects.

Skills \ Roles	Visionary	Ambassador user	Advisor User	Project Manager	Technical Co-ordinator	Team Leader	Senior Dev.	Developer	Facilitator	Scribe
Communication skills	√	√	√	√	√	√	√	√	√	√
Listener/ Interpreter	√					√	√	√	√	√
Mgmt. skills				√		√				
Motivation skills				√		√			√	
Politically aware		√		√						
Business aware	√	√	√	√		√	√	√	√	√
Practical business knowledge	√	√	√							
Technically aware				√	√	√	√	√	√	√
Tools skills						√	√	√		
Technical vision					√					
Skilled in techniques						√	√			
Analytical skills						√	√		√	
Familiar with standards					√	√	√	√		
Standards expert					√					
Wordsmith										√

The DSDM role/skills matrix

The various DSDM roles and the specific skills which are required to fulfil those roles are summarised in the role/skills matrix given above:

As a guide to selecting appropriate people from the IT department for the various DSDM roles where a developer is appropriate the following matrix shows DSDM roles that the an individual occupying a standard IT role could tackle.

Conventional IT Role \ DSDM Role	Exec Sponsor	Visionary	Ambas-sador User	Advisor User	Proj Mgr	Tech Co-ord	Team Leader	Senior Dev	Developer	Facilitator	Scribe
Analyst/Programmer						√	√	√	√		√
Business Analyst					√		√	√			√
Designer						√	√	√	√		√
Senior User Management	√	√									
System Architect						√					
Technical Specialist						√		√	√		
Users			√	√	√		√				√

Matrix Mapping Traditional IT Roles onto DSDM Team Roles

4 Successful Characteristics for a DSDM Team

To operate successfully a DSDM Team should be self-directed and highly motivated. The team should be small (six maximum) eliminating the communication problems faced by large teams and may be re-structured if the team is not being effective. The team should be made up of users and developers carrying equal responsibility within a team success culture where problems are team problems, not a cause for laying blame.

The team should consist of excellent communicators with informal but planned team meetings. It is also helpful if team members are physically in the same area of the organisation, at least while the project is enacted. It is the responsibility of the Project Manager to establish this communication environment.

As stated several times already user involvement is essential and can only be assured if:

- the **Executive Sponsor** secures co-operation of user managers;

- the **User Managers** are prepared to release staff for significant periods of time, even full time;

- the **Project Manager** controls user expectations.

Notes

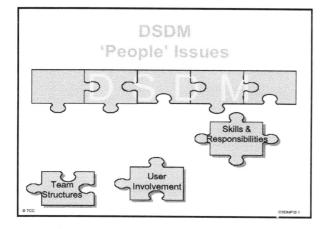

Build the right system
prototype
iterate
prioritise
evolutionary spec.

Active user involvement
ownership
• "no blame"

deliver a usable system on time

Frequent deliverables
visible progress
timebox deliverables

Empower DSDM teams
agree functionality
enact agreement

Notes

DSDM Teams, Roles and Skills

© TCC   DSDMP/2/4

DSDM Roles

The following roles are defined:

- Executive Sponsor (U)
- Visionary (U)

Other Specialist Roles

- Project Manager (U/D)

- Team Leader (D)
- Ambassador User (U)
- Advisor User (U)
- Developer/Senior Developer (D)

projects may merge some roles

- Technical Co-ordinator (D)

- Facilitator (U/D/Independent)
- Scribe (U/D)

© TCC   DSDMP/2/5

Executive Sponsor Role

Attributes:
- ability to commit funds and resources
- ability to question
- decisiveness
- political awareness
- business knowledge

Responsibilities:
- the 'owner' of the system with ultimate responsibility for it
- to make effective and rapid decisions
- respond to escalated issues
- ensure funds and resources are available as needed
- monitor business case
- commitment and availability throughout

© TCC   DSDMP/2/6

Notes

Ambassador User Role

Skills:
- good knowledge of the business area and politics
- high level view of how the system must function
- good communicator, able to pass on knowledge and ideas

Responsibilities:
- provide key user input to requirement/design sessions
- provide detail of business scenarios
- to gather user opinions and secure agreement
- to provide input to prototyping
- review documentation,
- review and accept delivered software
- provide user documentation and manage user training
- organise and control user testing

> Ambassador users must (*and must be seen to*) represent the whole user community, must be positive toward the development and be able to promote user opinion (confident to speak up)

© TCC DSDMP/2/7

Project Manager Role

Skills:
- good communicator
- plan and manage project
- politically aware
- business aware
- ability to solve technical and personnel problems

Responsibilities:
- report to management/steering committee
- plan and schedule project/monitor progress/manage risk
- target and motivate teams
- set team objectives
- chair project meetings
- manage user involvement/availability
- handle exceptions
- identify/call in specialist roles
- handle escalated project team problems

© TCC DSDMP/2/8

Developer/Senior Developer Role

Skills (Senior Developer):
- experience of prototyping techniques
- experience of tools and other techniques being used
- good listener/communicator
- good business area awareness

Skills (Developer):
- knowledge of prototyping techniques
- knowledge of tools and other techniques being used
- good listener/communicator
- business awareness

Responsibilities:
- create detailed documentation as necessary
- work with users to define business requirements, create prototypes
- create other components, such as a logical data model
- review/test personal work and that of others
- create test scripts
- review and test own and others' work

© TCC DSDMP/2/9

Notes

Team Management

Project Manager:

- is appointed by the team
- must understand the business issues
- must understand the technical issues
- must relate well to the users
- must facilitate decisions by the team if necessary (arbitrate not dictate)
- must appreciate the pressure which RAD teams are under and avoid 'burnout' of team members

© TCC   DSDMP/2/10

Specialists

Specialists brought in as required:
- business consultants
- technical consultants
- specialist in human factors
- configuration manager
- quality manager
- systems integrator
- operations co-ordinator
- support & maintenance specialist
  and many others ...!

© TCC   DSDMP/2/11

DSDM Teams

- self-directed
- small (no more than six)
- composed of users and developers with equal responsibility

- subject to re-structuring if team is not working

- underpinned by a team success approach/no blame ("anti-fault") culture

© TCC   DSDMP/2/12

Notes

Communication

Project Manager must establish:

- an environment conducive to good communication:

- team members who are good communicators

- team members physically located together

- planned informal team meetings

© TCC   DSDMP/2/ 13

User Involvement

Effective user involvement requires that:

the Executive Sponsor secures
co-operation of user managers

 the User Managers must be prepared
to release staff for significant periods of
time, even full time

the Project Manager must
control user expectations

© TCC   DSDMP/2/ 14

DSDM Roles and Teams

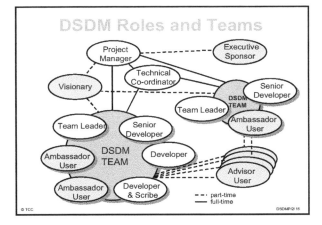

© TCC   DSDMP/2/ 15

Notes

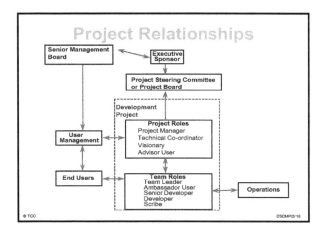

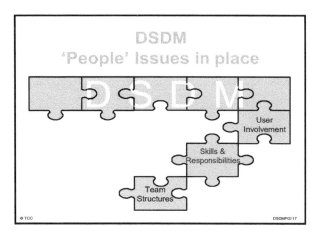

Visionary Role

Skills:
- excellent communicator
- extremely business aware
- very aware of technical options

Responsibilities:
- promote translation of vision into practice
- wider view of end-to-end process
- contribute to key requirement, design and review sessions
- resolve business area conflicts
- ensure availability of user resources
- monitor progress in line with original vision
- commitment and availability throughout

© TCC   DSDMP/2/18

Notes

Advisor User Role

Skills:
- practical knowledge of the business area
- able to communicate knowledge and ideas

Responsibilities:
- provide information on request
- practical input to prototyping and review process
- approve practicality of design and prototypes
- assist in business and usability testing

> Use of more than one individual in this role
> will bring wider experiences to bear on the project
> and encourage OWNERSHIP

© TCC   DSDMP/2/19

Technical Co-ordinator Role

Skills:
- experience of the tools
- experience of the standards
- senior technician who has seen the problems before
- good technical vision
- effective communicator

Responsibilities:
- determine the technical environment
- control configuration management procedures
- ensure adherence to standards of best practice
- advise on and co-ordinate each team's technical activities
- attend prototyping sessions to advise on standards
- ensure maintainability objectives are met
- agree and control the software architecture
- identify opportunities for reuse
- manage release control

© TCC   DSDMP/2/20

Team Leader Role

Skills:
- good communicator/listener
- technically competent
- business awareness
- analytical skills
- trained in techniques (facilitated workshops, prototyping ...)

Responsibilities:
- develop, maintain agreement to Business Area Definition
- ensure user requirements are addressed
- organise user/developer prototyping sessions
- encourage full participation of team members
- drive prototyping sessions to achieve objectives on time
- change control
- promote team well-being and motivation

© TCC   DSDMP/2/21

Notes

Facilitator Role

Skills:
- excellent inter-personal skills
- excellent communicator
- good presentation skills
- ability to be impartial
- competent in the workshop process
- business aware

Responsibilities:
- agree scope of workshop with project manager
- plan workshop
- familiarise self with business area
- interview participants
- facilitate workshop to meet objectives
- review workshop against objectives

© TCC   DSDMP/2/22

Scribe Role

Skills:

good communicator/listener
technically & business aware
good written communicator

Responsibilities:

record all points/actions relevant to the system
assist in interpretation of such documentation
project documentation distribution

© TCC   DSDMP/2/23

Session 3
Facilitated Workshops

1   Facilitated Workshops – what are they?

Workshops are meetings of a particular format, held to achieve quickly a particular purpose within a systems development project. They involve both end-user (customer) and IT staff and may be held to:

- obtain decisions;

- extract information;

- design aspects of the system;

- obtain agreement;

- establish commitment;

- secure approval.

A facilitated workshop is often the best technique for eliciting a key business or technical decision from a group of people, either within one organisation, or in some cases including partners and suppliers.

There are several areas where the technique can be used to generate high quality deliverables in a very short time scale:

- **Business Vision Analysis**: to help an organisation focus on and develop its vision and mission statement, which will provide a framework for its future business direction. From this statement, corporate objectives and goals can be determined for the key organisational units.

- **Business Systems Planning**: to help an organisation identify and plan for the development of future information systems to support the business objectives.

- **Business Process Design**: to help an organisation identify and design and prototype business processes which support the business objectives.

- **Business Information Systems Benefits**: to help an organisation determine where best to deploy its limited financial resources, to achieve maximum benefit to the business from its investment.

- **Information Systems Requirements Definition**: to help prepare an agreed definition of what facilities a new business information system should provide, together with their business priorities.

- **Information System Design**: to help define how the system requirements can be realised.

- **Technical System Options**: which can be applied in two situations:

  - to help define which technical option best satisfies a set of business requirements,

  - to perform a short term review on an existing project which requires an immediate re-focus in direction.

- **Acceptance Test Planning**: to help define how the Delivered System will be accepted by the users. This type of workshop will continue through a DSDM project, as each increment is produced.

A facilitated workshop is used for all objective-driven, decision-making workshops in a DSDM project. Often facilitated workshops are referred to as Joint Application Development (JAD) workshops within IT developments. Other RAD books and methods often differentiate between the earlier Joint Requirements Planning (JRP) workshops and the later Joint Application Design (JAD).

2. Facilitated Workshops and the RAD Lifecycle

The table on the following page shows the typical types of facilitated workshops which may be held during the DSDM life-cycle. Others may, of course, be used as needed.

These may be combined or sub-divided further, depending upon the project. Not all may form part of any particular project, and some may occur many times, with different deliverables. Some examples of typical facilitated workshops and their participants are given below.

At the outset of a project a Feasibility Report is produced. At the beginning of this phase, the **Information Systems Requirements Definition** workshop may take the form of several workshops, concerned specifically with establishing the objective in unambiguous terms, with scoping the development, and with outlining the requirements at a high level. (These are sometimes called **Scoping Workshops**). Such a workshop may define the system boundaries, elicit decisions about the new system and seek commitment and approval for the project. The results would then form a part of the Feasibility Report. The main participants in this initial Information Systems Requirements Definition Workshop are likely to be:

- the Executive Sponsor;

- Senior User Managers;

- Project Team Representatives;

- an <u>Independent</u> Facilitator.

DSDM Phase	Type of Facilitated Workshop
Feasibility Study	Information systems requirements definition
	Business information systems benefits
	Technical systems options
Business Study	Information systems requirements definition
	Business information systems benefits
	Business process design
	Requirements prioritisation
Functional Model Iteration	Information systems requirements definition (including prioritisation)
	Acceptance test planning
Design and Build Iteration	Information system design
	Technical systems options
Implementation	

Typical facilitated workshop types

Once the project is under way, an **Information Systems Requirements Definition Workshop** of a more detailed kind can be used to gather the full spectrum of user requirements and develop a High Level Data or object Model and a High Level Function Model. The scoping of the project allows the team to identify the classes of user needing to be added to the team. The participants are therefore:

- Senior User Managers;

- Nominated User Representatives;

- Project Team Representatives;

- an <u>Independent</u> Facilitator.

Several workshops in the form of **Information Systems Design Facilitated Workshop**s are used during design activities to develop Prototypes and feed back refinements to the requirements and system models if appropriate. Conversely they may feed back information which means that the functionality has to be modified and even de-scoped to meet the project timescales. The team at this stage must have Prototyping Tool Specialists within it and will consist of:

- Prototyping Tool Specialists;

- the Nominated User Representatives;

- Project Team Representatives;

- an Independent Facilitator.

Typically, a Facilitated Workshop session, at whatever stage it is used, will raise other issues, which are not the direct focus of that session. These issues are noted and may require further Facilitated Workshops to resolve them or reference back to the Executive Sponsor for resolution if the team feels that this is appropriate. It is naturally incumbent upon him to respond rapidly on such issues!

3 Suggested Workshop Roles and Responsibilities

3.1 Workshop Sponsor

The holder of this role is the **problem owner**, who needs the deliverable to be produced and has decision-making power over its completeness. Thus The Workshop Sponsor is often the Executive Sponsor. The Workshop Sponsor should be senior person, possibly a director, within the organisation, who has overall management responsibility for all users interested in the business area. He or she must be able to make decisions and resolve conflict and have the authority to approve expenditure of money and resource during the project.

The sponsor must be encouraged to attend at least the beginning and end of the key workshops to provide an introduction and receive a summary. If this is not possible, the sponsor must nominate an individual to represent the role who will have the necessary knowledge and empowerment, but must also command the respect of other users in the workshop.

3.2 Workshop Owner

The Workshop Owner is often the Project Manager. The Workshop Owner is responsible for setting the workshop objectives and determining the deliverables from the workshop. The Workshop Owner is responsible for the final deliverables from the workshop. The Workshop Owner works with the Facilitator to help re-plan the workshop if particular topics are taking longer than expected. The Workshop Owner identifies the workshop participants and ensures that all are represented in the workshop. The Visionary or, if present, the Executive Sponsor resolves conflicts and sets priorities. If the holder of neither role is present, the Workshop Owner takes on those responsibilities. The Workshop Owner is present throughout the workshop in order to emphasise the importance of the process.

3.3   Facilitator

DSDM Consortium Experience has shown that a Facilitator who is competent in the facilitated workshop process is key to workshop success. In order to be seen to be impartial, the Facilitator should be from a different business area from the project in question. The role of the Facilitator is to concentrate on the workshop process so that all participants have an equal opportunity to contribute. The main task of the Facilitator is to deal with all of the "people" aspects of the workshops by getting participants to work as a team. The Facilitator may document results and decisions on flip charts, for example, that act as "group memory". The Facilitator does not contribute to the content of the workshop.

3.4   Participants

Participants represent the views of the project stakeholders (e.g. the business and software development community). They are the individuals who are knowledgeable in the areas under consideration. They manage and operate the system and include managers, supervisors, clerical staff, and IT staff.

The participants in the group must have between them, the desire, authority, responsibility and knowledge to ensure that the right result is produced for the business. They must be empowered to agree decisions between themselves without reference outside the workshop.

Participants must have completed the necessary preparation and need to be committed to the workshop process.

3.5   Scribes

A *technical* Scribe captures all of the workshop outputs, such as requirements, perhaps using an appropriate software tool. The Facilitator is responsible for explaining technical models that the Scribe produces. The technical Scribe should be able to print out relevant parts of the model for review at various times.

A *commentary* Scribe summarises all the background discussion during the workshop. It is important that the person with this role has a good grounding in the project to ensure familiarity with issues, terminology and project background.

The type and number of scribes will be decided by the nature of the workshop.

The role of scribe is a key one, and should not be given lightly to the most junior member of the team. It is often the practice of project teams to rotate the scribe role between team members. This can work effectively, provided that continuity is provided between workshop sessions, and the appropriate level and style of documentation of the workshops is agreed beforehand.

3.6 Observers

Observers should be avoided wherever possible. Although they play no part in the proceedings, their presence may "cramp the style" of the team and prevent its effective working.

If observers are unavoidable seat them out of line of sight of the participants and ensure that they understand that they are there to observe, not to contribute. One example of a legitimate observer would be a trainee Facilitator, who would want to observe the group dynamics, without being part of the group.

3.7 Prototypers (if appropriate)

A highly competent technical specialist, who is capable of creating screens quickly, is needed for this role. A computer and appropriate software must be provided for them. If prototyping of screens is to take place during the workshop, a prototyper must attend the workshop.

4 The Format of Facilitated Workshops

Workshops may last a few hours or even days, depending upon the timescales of the project and the strength of project management which is necessary to organise intensive events such as a three or five-day workshop. Length will also depend upon the availability of appropriate attendees, whilst the number and nature of attendees will depend upon the task to be covered and the deliverable to be achieved. For example, for requirements capture, or entity model definition, many end-users may be needed to cover a wide business area, in addition to data analysis specialists from the IT department. It may be necessary for the workshop to break into smaller groupings to increase effectiveness, bringing their workshop products back to the larger forum later.

It is critical, especially for workshops lasting for a day or more, that the structure is carefully considered beforehand to ensure the best use of everyone's time.

5 Facilitated Workshop Activities

The activities associated with a Facilitated Workshop are:

- Plan the workshop (Workshop Definition);

- Prepare for the workshop;

- The Workshop Session:

  - run the workshop;

  - review the workshop;

- Document the workshop;

- Follow-up (Workshop Review).

5.1 Plan the Workshop

The Project Manager defines the objectives of the workshop; the attendees and what form the workshop should take. It may even be necessary to define several workshops to achieve the objectives. The size of the workshop should ideally be in the range of six to twelve people (more can be accommodated if necessary, but additional planning is required.).

5.2 Prepare for the Workshop

In preparation for the workshop, the facilitator must circulate information to the participants so that they fully understand the objective of the workshop and the background to it. The workshop agenda detailing when, where and who will be attending as well as the order of proceedings will be sent out together with any pre-workshop reading. In particular, individuals will be advised where their input to the workshop is needed so that they may prepare beforehand the information that they need to make an effective contribution.

5.3 Run the Workshop

The tight timescales of a DSDM project mean that the workshop needs to maintain its focus and therefore the facilitator must run a 'tight ship' at a brisk pace. Some facilitators operate on the principle of the *five-minute rule* wherein any disagreement that can not be resolved in a period of five minutes is declared an 'open issue'. Such open issues are documented and deferred to a later session or to the Executive Sponsor as described above.

The workshop has a number of defined roles in DSDM:

- the **Project Manager** who will be present throughout the workshop to underscore the importance of the process;

- the **Facilitator**, a role which is crucial to the success of the workshop. It is essential to have a competent qualified leader of the workshop, someone who is trained and experienced in the role. It is the Facilitator who ensures that all participants are given the opportunity to contribute to the work of the Facilitated Workshop. Team building also falls to the facilitator of a Facilitated Workshop who may document main points on a whiteboard/flipchart pad as the workshop progresses. The facilitator <u>does NOT contribute to the content</u> of the workshop, the role being very much one of 'oiling the wheels' of progress;

- the **Participants** are representatives of the identified classes of user together with IT staff;

- the **Scribe** role must be covered by someone technically able to document workshop products perhaps using a software tool. These will later be printed for comment and review or as input to future sessions. There is also a need to record the discussion content of the workshop and recording open issues as required. This may require a second person to cover this aspect of the role. At the end of the meeting the scribe will read back to the participants, the main decisions and actions that have come out of the workshop.

Observers may attend the workshop to pick up background information on the project but they have no active role in the workshop.

For workshops to be effective there are a few basic guidelines which the facilitator should remind people of at the the beginning of the Facilitated Workshop and elsewhere if it should become necessary:

- start on time – a RAD project requires that all timescales are constrained;

- respect the views of others;

- if participants do not speak up then they will be assumed to have agreed the point under discussion;

- anarchy can not rule – one speaker at a time;

- the team must maintain its focus.

5.4   Review the Workshop

The quality of the workshop has to be examined and any lessons learnt fed back into the operation of future workshops. In particular, did the workshop meet its objectives fully or only partially and did all participants contribute to the process? Most importantly how effective did the participants feel that the workshop had been and did it run to time?

5.5   Document the Workshop

The scribe produces and distributes a Workshop Report <u>very soon after the workshop</u>. It is sent to all participants and under instruction of the Project Manager to other interested parties (not participants) who will be affected by the products of the workshop.

The Workshop Report documents:

- decisions taken;

- actions and against whom they are assigned;

- open issues;

- requirements details;

- design details;

- function models;

- data models.

5.6 Follow-up

The Executive Sponsor and Workshop Sponsor must be consulted to confirm satisfaction with the workshop's results. All actions marked for follow-up activity outside the workshop forum must be addressed not just documented!

6 Benefits of Facilitated Workshops

Facilitated Workshops are a quick way of eliciting information, compared to widespread interviewing, and provide a forum for the resolution of differences of opinion and conflict of information. They give a sense of involvement to participants (team building) and as such gain acceptance for the developing system (ownership). However it is essential that the key decision-makers are involved and that the workshops are empowered to make decisions about the direction of the developing system otherwise progress will be hampered. By bringing people together from a number of business areas in a Facilitated Workshop a broader perspective of the business is created. Understanding is therefore improved and better decisions can be made for the business, as participants 'bounce ideas' off eachother creating a more effective and productive outcome. Clear policy guidelines are needed to ensure a clear decision-making framework for the workshop members.

7 Success Factors for Facilitated Workshops

The factors which have been found, in practice, to greatly improve the success of Facilitated Workshops are:

- a good, trained facilitator (workshop leader);

- flexibility in the format of different workshops, but clearly defined objectives;

- thorough preparation before the workshop;

- a mechanism for ensuring that previous workshops' results are built in;

- a solution or agreement should not be forced. If the workshop participants cannot agree on a point (perhaps due to lack of information) within the workshop, the leader should recommend action to remedy the shortfall outside of the workshop structure;

● much can be learned by scheduling a short review session at the end of each workshop and documenting the plus and minus points of the workshop;

● participants should receive details of the decisions and actions soon after the workshop;

● with experience, it should be assessed whether workshops suit the culture of the organisation, and whether this method of finding facts and making decisions is acceptable to the organisation.

Notes

FACILITATED WORKSHOPS

JOINT APPLICATION DEVELOPMENT
(JAD)
WORKSHOPS

© TCC

DSDMP/3/1

Facilitated
Workshops

© TCC

DSDMP/3/2

What is a
Facilitated Workshop?

- A place where a specific job of work is done …

- and a product produced.

© TCC

DSDMP/3/3

Notes

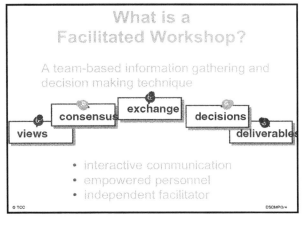

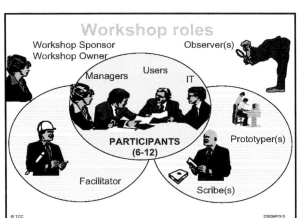

Notes

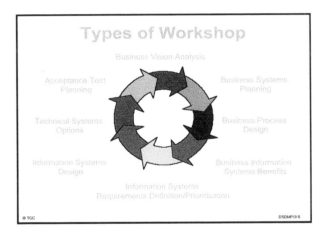

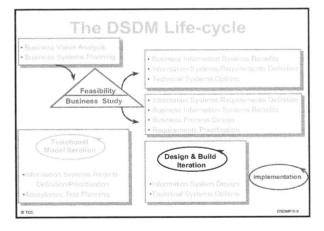

Notes

Information Systems Requirements
Definition Workshop

OBJECTIVES:

• Boundaries

• Decision

• Commitment

• Approval

© TCC   DSDMP/3/10

An Example of an Information Systems
Requirements Definition (Scoping) Workshop

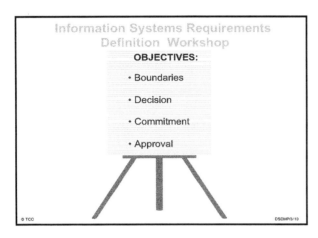

WHO

Senior User Managers   Project Team Representatives

Sponsor (Owner)   **Independent** Facilitator

Scoping Workshop

•Scope
•Exclusions
•Issues
•Timetable
•Requirements
•Scoping Data Model

Feasibility Report

© TCC   DSDMP/3/11

Activities within a typical Workshop

Identify Requirements

Identify required data

Identify required Functions

Identify Triggers

Link Functions to Triggers

Logical Data Model

Requirements

Refine Model

Function Hierarchies

Triggers

Issues

© TCC   DSDMP/3/12

Notes

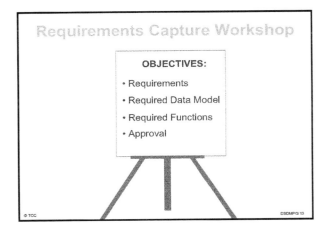

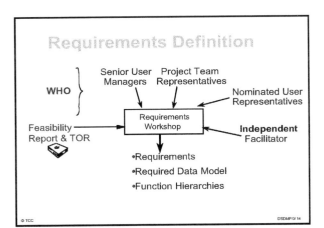

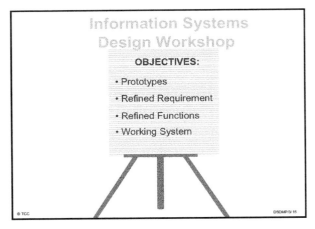

Notes

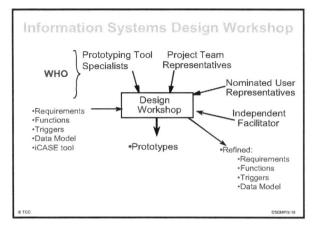

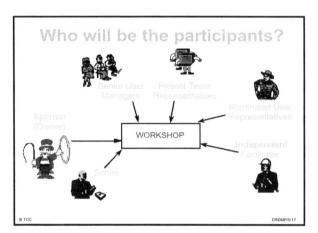

Workshop Activities

- Workshop Definition
- Prepare for Workshop

- Run Workshop session
- Review Workshop deliverables

- Final Document - Workshop Report
- Workshop Review with Workshop Sponsor

© TCC   DSDMP/3/18

Notes

Planning a Workshop

* WHY   - Define objectives and deliverables

* WHO   - Participants and roles

* HOW MANY - How many workshops?

* WHAT   - What form should the workshop take?

* WHERE   - Suitable venue

* WHEN   - Right time. How long?

© TCC   DSDMP/3/19

Prepare for Workshop

• Workshop Objectives

• Required deliverables

• Information circulated beforehand?

• Agenda

© TCC   DSDMP/3/20

Why set an Agenda?

• aids thinking

• logical sequence

• keeps meeting on track

• guides participants

• identifies information needs

© TCC   DSDMP/3/21

Notes

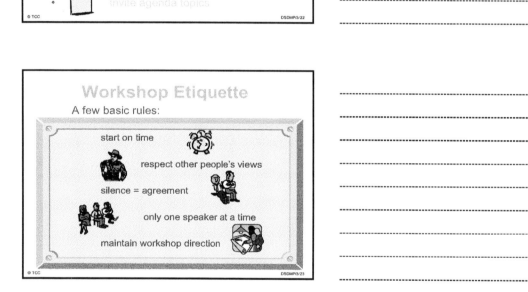

Notes

Success Factors

- Good Facilitator, trained for the job
- Flexibility of format but NOT objectives
- Preparation
- Education (Preparation session before Workshop)

  - Earlier results built in
  - User solution facilitated, not forced
  - Review of good/bad points
  - Feedback of Results to participants

- Suitability of Workshops to organisational culture

© TCC   DSDMP/3/25

Session 4
DSDM Project Management Issues

1 Introduction

In this session on Project Management within DSDM we shall discuss the fundamental differences between traditional project management and DSDM project management as well as the major project management issues of risk, estimating, configuration management, quality and testing.

Some of the issues that a project manager has to consider, such as team management structure and user involvement, have been discussed in the earlier sessions. Others such as timeboxing and the management of prototyping will be discussed later. Estimating, although mentioned in this session, will be subject to further discussion along with timeboxing.

2 Traditional v. DSDM Project Management

Traditional system development methods are based upon the philosophy that they will focus upon a fixed specification delivering **all** functionality specified therein by controlling resource levels to keep the project development on schedule and within budget.

If the system:

● **fails to meet the specification** then it is the fault of the developers;

● **fails to meet the business need** then it is the fault of the users...

...Someone is always to blame!

DSDM however follows a path through evolutionary change to the specification within a co-operative user-developer relationship where 'no-blame' is apportioned, where overriding responsibility is held by the team not the individual. Ultimate responsibility and accountability does however rest with an individual, the Executive Sponsor. It is down to the Executive Sponsor to ensure that <u>the doors to 'user availability' are firmly wedged open</u>. The objective is "...to deliver a usable system on time". Building the right system to meet the business need is of **primary** importance. The key to DSDM project management is to maximise business benefit by delivering essential functionality within tight timescales by controlling how much is developed rather than extending the time allotted.

DSDM achieves its objectives by:

● prototyping;

- iterative development;

- focusing on high priority functions which will deliver maximum business benefit;

- active user involvement;

- insisting on empowerment of the team;

- frequent delivery.

Much of the success of DSDM in action depends upon good communication, achieved by selection of the right team members, by keeping the team small and by the informal but planned meetings, which the team hold. The project manager has responsibility for monitoring progress and producing a weekly update report for management thus widening the element of communication. Where a large project has been broken down into several DSDM teams, this weekly report also may serve to keep the teams informed of eachother's progress.

3 The Major Issues

The major project management issues that will be covered here are:

- risk;

- estimating;

- configuration management;

- quality;

- testing.

3.1 Risk

There are risks to any system development project but for the DSDM process some risks are related to **The 9 principles.** Whatever the risk there are two aspects to it:

- recognise the risk;

- handle it with ownership, countermeasures, insurance, reduction or acceptance.

Most procurers of IT systems are concerned with two risks: that the system will not meet the needs of the business and that the project will overrun on time and/or cost. DSDM is designed to counteract both of these risks. Systems that meet the needs of the business are delivered through the incremental and iterative approach with its continuous feedback from users. Cost and time overruns are avoided by the use of timeboxes. Initially the focus will be on the DSDM principles and the consequences of the project not meeting those principles. Such risks are:

3.1.1 The necessary level of user involvement is not present.

DSDM requires an integrated team of developers and business staff, preferably co-located where the system will be used. Anything less than this constitutes a serious risk to successful implementation. At the outset of the project, time must be invested in identifying, and securing, the right level of involvement of the right users. It can be easy to get users into the project full-time when the eventual users are numbered in hundreds, but this gives rise to the problem of choosing the right representatives and selling the results to the rest of the user population. If the user population is small, it may be impossible to take key users away from their day-to-day work for more than a few hours a week. Whatever the level of user involvement, unless it is full-time, it is essential to fix regular times in staff's diaries when the project will be given first priority, as well as allowing for more ad-hoc contact as required.

A particular and very high risk occurs if the level of user involvement that was agreed at the start of the project is not forthcoming, or diminishes as the project progresses. In this case the issue needs to be escalated urgently to the Executive Sponsor and resolved to everyone's satisfaction.

3.1.2 The time spent in decision-making endangers the project schedule

If the level of empowerment is not understood by the development teams, it can lead to fear of overstepping the boundaries of responsibility and hence the activities slow down. The empowerment levels should be clearly stated in each person's terms of reference at the start of the project. Decisions on policy should be separated from operational decisions and, where policy decisions are referred to higher authorities, there needs to be a fast approval process

3.1.3 Team members become focused on activities rather than products

Risks begin to multiply when the length of a timebox is set arbitrarily and the development team becomes more absorbed by its activities than by the delivery of useful products.

These risks are best avoided by careful team selection, appropriate reward and recognition systems and by setting short timeboxes with very clearly-defined deliverable products.

3.1.4 Deliverables are not fit for their business purpose

Deliverables may either be over-engineered and thus take longer to build than necessary. Otherwise they may be insufficiently engineered. In the former case, the developers (often assisted by the Ambassador Users) can spend too much time is in enhancing the user interface unnecessarily. Having a well-defined Style Guide will limit unnecessary creativity in this area. In the latter case, lack of user involvement and/or timescales which are, or have become, too tight may be the problem.

It is a good idea to expect the team members to report progress by delivery against objectives rather than discussing how far through a particular task they are. This helps to produce the right mindset within the team.

Regular formal reviews should be held inside the team where deliverables are assessed against the minimum usable subset and against the business benefits expected from a particular deliverable. The business objectives should be revisited to ensure that the project is moving in the right direction.

3.1.5 Iterative and incremental development activities are not well controlled

A particular risk associated with iterative and incremental development is that of creeping functionality that does not converge to a working system. The ability to change one's mind is a cornerstone of value in DSDM, but it is also a weakness if the team cannot get closure on the delivery of a useful product. Short timeboxes, appropriate reward mechanisms and properly focused staff are keys to avoiding this trap. Additionally, frequent access to key user management helps if closure is needed.

3.1.6 Backtracking is difficult or even impossible

It is often tempting to implement an increment of development without providing the ability to fall back to an earlier version if the enhancement needs to be withdrawn. This constitutes a major risk and is why configuration management is stressed in DSDM. Good version control tools and standards are needed to avoid the problem.

Because configuration management can be labour intensive and time consuming, it is recommended that the development process is audited frequently to ensure compliance.

3.1.7 The high-level requirements are not baselined

A failure to baseline high-level requirements at the outset of the project is likely to lead to creeping functionality and timebox overruns. In some ways, this risk is greatest when the team is empowered and the users are fully involved. Grouping the requirements into modules that correspond to timeboxes is a powerful way to freeze the scope of all but the next timebox before moving into greater detail on that timebox.

3.1.8 Testing is not integrated throughout the lifecycle

If a system has high user involvement, then testing throughout the lifetime of the project is the natural way to progress. However, this testing may be informal and poorly recorded, unless thought is given to this at the start of the timebox. This will help formalise the testing and ensure that it is done thoroughly.

One risk management approach is to make one member of the team **Testing Champion**, with responsibility for ensuring that all necessary testing is both carried out and documented to the required level.

3.1.9 Not all stakeholders are committed to a collaborative and co-operative approach

Large-scale computer systems often involve a wide range of stakeholders, including suppliers and vendors. In these cases, the development team can have to handle a broad range of contractual terms and conditions. Where a fully collaborative state is not possible, the team should build in reviews to mitigate risks as and when required.

Where purchasing contracts apply, DSDM recommends a "time and materials" approach to labour procurement rather than a fixed cost approach, where possible.

An adversarial approach to deciding development activities, changes in scope, requirement priorities, etc. must be avoided. As soon as this occurs, communication and decision channels become rigid and the close partnership, which is essential to DSDM's success, is lost.

Other risks that are not directly related to DSDM principles include:

3.1.10 DSDM is not wholly applicable

It is strongly recommended that a risk assessment should be performed at the outset of every project, starting with the Suitability Filter A formal risk assessment should then be made and updated with every iteration of the Functional Model.

3.1.11 The development team does not understand the development process

If the developers are unfamiliar with the process, in-depth training needs to be carried out before the project begins. If the users are new to DSDM, it is worth spending a day training them at the beginning of the project. The user training should cover not only those who are to be part of the development team but their managers. This will also minimise a common problem in RAD projects, that of users committing, say, 70% of their time to the project and still being required to perform 50% or more of their normal job.

3.1.12 The organisation of the user area will change dramatically as a result of the introduction of the system

If the users in the project may not be those eventually involved with the finished product, then the project needs to be certain that the users in the project are willing and capable of participating in development. It is likely that staff who feel threatened by change will not participate as wholeheartedly as DSDM requires.

3.1.13 The original project approach turns out to be inappropriate during development

The understanding of the project is built up over a period of time and it is possible that the project may become too large to manage within the DSDM framework and the team as initially set up. If at any point DSDM is not appropriate the option to move out of DSDM and into another more suitable approach should be taken.

3.1.14 The development tool-set does not truly support incremental delivery

If the tools and techniques selected for development of the software are not designed for a RAD approach, this may cause significant delays to the development team. Tools must also be readily usable by the whole team in order for all team members to be certain that they are working on the correct version at any one time.

3.1.15 The development environment is unfamiliar to the developers

There is no provision in DSDM for the steep learning curves of skill acquisition in tool use in the project. Developers are expected to be familiar with the vast majority of the components of the development environment before the DSDM project begins. This includes everything related to development activities and control, such as hardware, tools, techniques, standards, and configuration management procedures. Where new areas of expertise are necessary, specialist support should be arranged at the start of the project to be available on demand.

3.2 Estimating in DSDM

Estimating is the subject of a later session and therefore for the moment it is sufficient to state that, unlike other methods, DSDM takes into account the level of user effort since user involvement is integral. What estimating in DSDM does not do is to build in a level of contingency for slippage (functionality is descoped timescale is fixed) or allow time for skill acquisition by the team.

3.3 Configuration Management

Configuration Management is:

'the process of identifying and defining the configuration items of a system, controlling the release and change of those items throughout the lifecycle recording and reporting status of configuration items and change requests and verifying completeness and correctness of configuration items'

ANSI/IEEE 729-1983.

Systems pass through a number of changes during their lifetime and it is essential that the changes are documented and the previous version(s) retained.

Change control is the set of formal procedures that enable changes to be made to configuration items and record the changes.

In DSDM products are developed and then through iteration are improved upon. There are potentially many individual products at on average three stages of development. The integrated completed system is also subject to configuration management. The overriding tenet is that all components of the system should be available if required, both current versions and previous ones. There may even be versions of software for different operating systems which have to be tracked.

Configuration Management thus has to be done because:

- DSDM is dynamic;

- iteration implies change which must be managed;

- all changes must be reversible – version control;

- developers need to be confident that they are working with both the same and current versions of aspects of the system.

Clearly Configuration Management is an extremely important task for DSDM. So who is responsible for doing it? Quite simply, the team must ensure that previous versions of the development products and associated documentation are retained and lodged in a previously defined storage area. The team, of course, is under extreme pressure and for this reason tool support and the skill to use it are essential. Whatever CM tool is used, it needs to have update and create restrictions since all the developers should have access to all of the developing configuration items. The parallel working which is inherent in DSDM must not result in concurrent development of the same Configuration Item. The tool must lock out developers from working on the same configuration item at the same time.

To monitor the process, a Configuration Management Champion (sometimes the term Project Librarian might be used) should be elected from the team. Obviously as DSDM development is so dynamic the Configuration Management process has to be on going throughout the project.

What, then, should be subject to Configuration Management? Whilst **as much as possible should be managed** the most obvious Configuration Items are the requirements, at each stage of their evolution, the dynamic system models, and each iteration of a prototype. The final agreed prototype is passed onto the next phase as a controlled set. A prototype configuration item will consist of the prototype itself, the tests run on it and a record of the user comments/test results.

The benefit of good configuration management is that it will allow future change impact analysis to be assessed. For example if the size of an entity attribute is changed, what screens, reports etc will be affected?

Configuration Management procedures have to be in place long before the project commences, there is no time in a DSDM project for its development 'on the fly'.

3.4 Quality Issues

Quality has been defined as:

- 'Fitness for Purpose'

and it has also been said that

- 'Quality has to be built in, it can not be inspected into a product'

There are however three aspects to quality which are directed toward the development of a quality product:

- quality control;

- quality assurance;

- quality management (and a QM system).

3.4.1 Quality Control

Quality Control is essentially the testing and rejection of faulty products. In DSDM the quality control is performed informally by the team with a formal inspection being carried out on the key *Business Area Definition* and *Prioritised Functions* documents.

DSDM quality control is achieved by

- inspection & review against DSDM product descriptions;

- dynamic testing of all software products;

- user review/demonstration of key prototypes;

- use of static code analysis tools if available.

3.4.2 Quality Assurance

Quality Assurance is the area where products are defined and their quality criteria established in preparation for quality control application.

There is yet another aspect of a DSDM project which must be subject to quality assurance and control and that is the application of the method itself. The areas of the method of focus for Quality Assurance are:

- is user involvement REALLY operating?

- are the users really empowered?

- is the lifecycle being followed?

- is feedback from reviews being incorporated?

- is back-tracking allowed, when necessary?

- are priorities being adhered to?

- are timeboxes being respected?

3.4.3   Quality Management

ISO 9000-3 on quality management appears to be contradictory in its message at least as far as DSDM is concerned.

It states:

This International Standard is intended for application irrespective of the lifecycle model used.

but goes on to say that:

In order to proceed with software development, the supplier should have a complete, unambiguous set of functional requirements.

This latter statement is at odds with the DSDM approach. However expert interpretation of it summarises the meaning to be:

"...say what you are going to do,

do it,

demonstrate that you have done it..."

and that is what DSDM sets out to do!

3.5   Testing in DSDM

As stated before testing is inter-threaded throughout the DSDM lifecycle. The six principles of testing in DSDM are:

- **Validation – meeting business requirements**: the performance of the system is measured against the baselined documents which state what it is expected to do. User team members will be involved throughout in this activity;

● **Benefit-directed**: this is giving priority to testing the areas of the system which will deliver key business benefits;

● **Error-centric**: the principle is that the purpose of testing is to find errors. A successful test is one which finds an error, which is then fixed, elevating the confidence of the team in the system;

● **Done throughout entire lifecycle**: all software products at all stages of the DSDM development process are tested;

● **Independent Testers**: testing should be performed by someone other than the software's author since this has been demonstrated to be more effective. The software's author will make all of the same assumptions during testing that were made during development. An independent tester will not;

● **Repeatable Tests**: tests, test data and test results are all included as configuration items within Configuration Management since at a later stage in the development it may be necessary to re-run the tests. These repeated tests may be used to test a modified version of the product for which the tests were designed for example.

The short timescale of a DSDM project means that documentation of tests should be at a reduced level aided by test tool support if at all possible. The purpose is to devise focused tests which are benefit directed, and therefore skilled testers are essential. Quality is important not quantity!

Finally, on testing, a key feature is to ensure that the purpose of testing is clearly defined before the test. At some points (e.g. initial iteration of a prototype) the testing may be to ensure that the expected information has been gleaned, rather than that anything is actually working and producing results. At the final iteration of a prototype (consolidation) it is likely that expected results can be defined, to be tested for. The different types of prototype, usability, business, capability/technique and performance/capacity impact on the expected results of testing and it is essential that the team are aware of just what type, or types, of prototype they are dealing with.

3.6   Maintenance

It is often asked if a system developed in a Rapid Application Development environment will have poor maintainability which in turn results in a high maintenance overhead (you'll pay for it in the long run!).

A well-developed system, whatever the development method, will require less maintenance than a poorly developed one. But as stated elsewhere, much of the maintenance effort is directed toward correcting developer misconceptions about user requirements. DSDM's total commitment to user involvement incorporates user business requirements during the development process eliminating much of the maintenance problem. Testing to detect errors is performed early and throughout the development process. Detection of errors early is much more cost-effective compared to late detection (Barry Boehm).

The issue of maintenance is also subject to a policy decision which is made by senior management whereby any one of three approaches may be taken:

- **maintainability is a requirement** for the new system and must be incorporated in line with the organisation's standards;

- **maintainability is not an issue** since the system is to have a short life, being replaced before the cost of maintenance becomes an issue;

- **maintainability is secondary** to rapid delivery of functionality, the business will accept the additional cost of subsequent re-engineering.

Maintainability in a DSDM project is due to four factors, all of which should be in place before the project commences:

- **Tools**: the use of tools to cover such areas as configuration management, testing and impact analysis aids maintainability;

- **People**: the people issues affecting maintainability are the development team skills, experience and business knowledge, user contribution and the maintenance team skills and motivation;

- **Documentation**: a level of documentation consistent with maintainability but also with the installation guide is needed.

- **Good practice guidelines**: these are important for DSDM projects to meet their maintainability objectives. The three key guidelines are the Generic Lifecycle Process Model for the installation, the Style Guide and the Internal Design Architecture. The Generic Model identifies the steps to be done, the tools to be used and the documentation to be produced. The Style Guide promotes a similar look and feel for a set of different applications that have the front end visible to the users across the business. The Internal Design Architecture identifies what the internal components of a system are and how they are composed by covering such items as coding standards, naming conventions, data architecture, reuse and error-handling.

Maintainability can be assured through **reuse** of components which have previously demonstrated their maintainability

3.7 Reuse

Reuse of components from different system developments, as well as improving maintainability by use of modular well tested units, carries a number of **benefits** consistent with DSDM:

- faster system delivery;

- higher development productivity;

- improved quality with higher levels of usability and reliability.

DSDM recognises that for successful reuse of components the correct environment must be present in the organisation. Therefore reuse is <u>an option</u> for achieving the DSDM project objectives in a short time frame with the team being responsible for (or for not) adopting reuse on the basis of cost/benefit judgement.

So what is the right environment? Quite simply it is where the organisational culture encourages reuse, where there is a reuse team which educates and promotes the reuse of components and where there is technical support for reuse (eg component repository, tool support for finding and accessing components, data dictionaries, CASE tools).

What sort of components can be reused? Clearly many components may be reusable although reuse is easier if the component was originally designed in a general way with reuse in mind. The sorts of components that can be reused are, for example:

- Design models (e.g. data models, object models, process models);

- Data dictionaries (e.g. data item definitions);

- Object-oriented application frameworks and class libraries;

- Component libraries (eg device drivers);

- Program module libraries;

- User Interface Style Guide elements (e.g. standard controls or images);

- Test scripts and data.

Reuse in DSDM is possible within all phases associated with system development:

- **Feasibility Study**: reuse has implications upon project feasibility itself and therefore the team must assess how costs, schedules and risks are affected by reuse. Existing models such as corporate data models and function hierarchies may be reused here;

- **Business Study**: existing models, such as corporate data models, provide a depth of knowledge about the business and should if possible be used (and even be enhanced) by the DSDM team;

- **Functional Model Iteration**: reuse of application frameworks, class libraries etc. can shortcut development here. Corporate style guides built into reusable components can shortcut development of usable interfaces;

- **Design and Build Iteration**: development can be more productive through the use of application frameworks, class libraries, component libraries etc. Where new development takes place, components should be designed to integrate with reuse components such that they too may become part of the reuse library. Testing can reuse test data which has proven to be effective on other projects.

Implicit in the discussion above is that reuse components, by virtue of their repeated use, will themselves pass through an iterative cycle of development. These components will thus need to be subject to configuration management where the implications of any changes must be considered. In turn this means that not all aspects of reuse are cost saving and beneficial.

If reuse is to be encouraged the organisation's infrastructure must support a reuse library with configuration management of its archives. These incur a cost. However this library is a corporate asset which will provide benefits overall, not just for DSDM projects, and therefore support costs for the library are <u>outside</u> any DSDM project costings. Yet other potential risks of reuse are concerned with:

- inappropriate selection of reuse components which require extensive rework;

- an extended project time frame due to familiarisation of the team with reuse components to make selection of viable components.

However once a reuse policy is in place the benefits can begin to accrue, these benefits becoming ever more tangible as teams become familiar with the reuse resources available to them.

Notes

Project Management for DSDM

© TCC

DSDMPI/4/1

Session Objectives

• Traditional v. DSDM Project Management

• Major Project Management Issues

© TCC

DSDMPI/4/2

Traditional v. DSDM Project Management

Traditional:
• strict adherence to specification
• control of resource

...in order to hit time & budget for the fixed specification

DSDM:
• evolutionary change to specification
• co-operative, 'no-blame' user/developer relationship
• timeboxing

...to deliver a usable system on time

© TCC

DSDMPI/4/3

Notes

Major Issues

Risk

Estimating

Configuration Management

Quality

Testing

Maintenance (& reuse)

© TCC   DSDMP/4/4

Risk of using DSDM

lack of necessary level of consistent user involvement

time spent in decision-making endangers the project schedule

focus on activities rather than products

deliverables not fit for purpose

iteration is not well-controlled

backtracking difficult or impossible

high-level requirements not baselined

testing not integrated throughout the life cycle

co-operative collaboration is not everyone's agenda

DSDMP/4/5

Other Risks

- DSDM not wholly applicable

- Development team does not understand development process

- User organisation dramatically affected by new system

- Project becomes non-applicable to DSDM

- Development tools do not support incremental delivery

- Development team not familiar with development environment

© TCC   DSDMP/4/6

Notes

Should

- take account of the level of user effort

.....but should NOT

- build in time contingency (timescale **will not** slip!)
- allow familiarisation time (use **skilled** developers!)

© TCC   DSDMP/4/7

Configuration Management

What is Configuration Management?

The process of **identifying and defining**
the configuration items of a system,
controlling the release and change
of those items throughout the
lifecycle **recording and reporting**
status of configuration items and change requests
and **verifying completeness and correctness** of
configuration items   ANSI/IEEE 729 -1983

Change Control = set of formal procedures
    which record and enable changes to configuration items.

© TCC   DSDMP/4/8

Configuration Management

Why is CM necessary?

- DSDM is dynamic
- iteration implies change which must be managed
- all changes must be reversible - version control
- developers need to be confident of right version

CM Champion

- Tech. Co-ordinator?
- within team

Tool Support?

© TCC   DSDMP/4/9

Notes

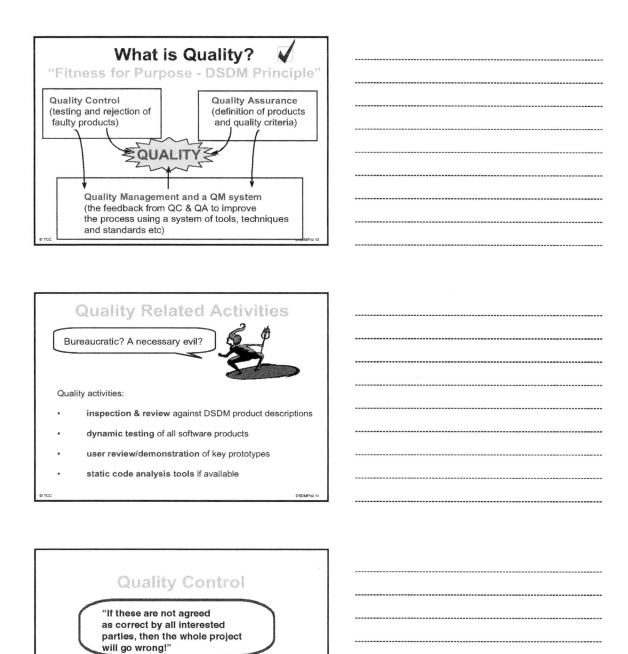

Notes

Quality Assurance in DSDM

DSDM projects can satisfy ISO 9001 TickIT

DSDM minimises the number of intermediate products for QA

DSDM Quality Audit focuses on the key areas:
- is user involvement there?
- are users really empowered
- is life-cycle being followed?
- is feedback from prototyping reviews being incorporated?
- is backtracking allowed when necessary?
- are priorities being adhered to?
- are timeboxes being respected?

© TCC   DSDMP/4/13

Quality Management

" ...say what you are going to do,

do it,

demonstrate that you have done it... "

© TCC   DSDMP/4/14

DSDM Testing Principles

Validation - fit for business purpose

Benefit-directed

Error-centric

Testing throughout entire life-cycle

Repeatable Testing

Independent Testing

© TCC   DSDMP/4/15

Notes

Approach to Testing

Short timescales of DSDM Projects impose:

- reduced documentation of tests

- requirement for skilled testers

- benefit directed test selection criterion

- need for tool support

© TCC　　　　　　　　　　　　　　　　　　DSDMP/4/16

Objectives of Testing

Prototype Category	Investigative	Refining	Consolidating
Business	EI	EI/ER	ER
Usability	EI	EI/ER	ER
Performance	EI	EI/ER	ER
Capability	EI	EI	EI

EI　　　= Expected Information
EI/ER = Expected Result

© TCC　　　　　　　　　　　　　　　　　　DSDMP/4/17

Maintenance - What does RAD mean?

Poor Maintainability?

High Maintenance Overhead Cost?

© TCC　　　　　　　　　　　　　　　　　　DSDMP/4/18

Notes

Maintainability v Cost

Senior Management decision at outset:

☑ maintainability a requirement for the new system

OR

☑ maintainability is not a problem: short system life, replaced before maintenance an issue

OR

☑ maintainability secondary to rapid delivery
The business will accept cost of re-engineering

© TCC   DSDMPI4/19

Reuse

Benefits:
   faster system delivery

   increased productivity

   better quality (more usable, maintainable & reliable system

Costs/Risks:
   cost of library/configuration management of reuse components

   inappropriate component selection

   project time extended by familiarisation time required

© TCC   DSDMPI4/20

Reuse

Of what:
   design models - eg data, process models
   data dictionary definitions
   component library
   test data/scripts

When to reuse in DSDM:
   Feasibility
   Business Study
   Functional Model Iteration
   Design and Build Iteration

© TCC   DSDMPI4/21

Notes

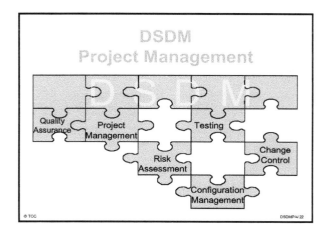

Session 5
Timeboxing and Estimating

Timeboxing

"Creative people in many walks of life have a deadline. A magazine writer, television producer or seminar developer creates material for a certain date. Whatever else happens, he must not fail to meet the deadline.

To meet the deadline, he may allow the contents to slip. There may be items he wants to include but cannot do so in time. The producer of a television documentary or a seminar broadcast by satellite may say "I wish I could have interviewed so-and-so" or "I wish we had better footage on this". However, there is no time to obtain the extra interview or footage. The deadline is absolute. The show must go on the air. There is much similarity between television production and the building of information systems. Television production employs a planning phase, design and storyboarding, then construction. A difference is that most Information System (IS) development does not have a firm deadline. Sometimes developers claim for a year that the system is "95% complete".

James Martin 1991

1   Introduction

The purpose of timeboxing is to control the amount of time taken to complete a piece of work, and to maximise the effectiveness of the effort spent.

In this session we shall look at the key characteristics of timeboxing, the main project management requirements for success, and recommended approach to timeboxing.

2   What is a Timebox?

Timeboxing is an essential aspect of DSDM projects. It allows the iterative nature of the work to be controlled and deliverables to be produced on time.

There are several definitions of timeboxes used within DSDM. One is that the whole timespan between the start-date and end-date of the project is a timebox. Within this, further time-boxes can be defined. These provide a series of fixed deadlines by which intermediate products will be completed.

3 Reasons for Timeboxing

Timeboxing was first used by Dupont Fibres, who restricted their development to 90 days. They later extended this to 120 days, to allow time for project close-down and documentation completion.

Timeboxing prevents "creeping functionality" often found in prototyping situations and the tendency of the development not to converge to a working system. It prevents the "95% complete" syndrome where, from the point in time when developers feel that their development is "95% complete" it takes as long again to actually complete!

4 Key Characteristics of Timeboxing

The key feature of timeboxing is that the amount of work to be done does not dictate the time actually taken, but rather the time available dictates what can be done.

In all cases, when the deadline expires, a review of the state of the project must be held, at which the project leader defines the achievements and reaffirms the scope of the project. Any work which had been intended for completion in the timebox, but which was not completed must be reconsidered, re-prioritised and replanned. This will have an impact on all subsequent timeboxes.

This obviously represents a profound change from the more traditional approach in systems development, where estimates and delivery dates tend to be extended as the work progresses. Timeboxing is designed to prevent exactly that sort of drift.

4.1 The MoSCoW Rules

In order to ensure that a timebox **will** finish on time, there has to be some flexibility in the deliverables it must achieve. If there is no flexibility, estimates must be perfect and nothing unforeseen must delay progress (a situation which represents an impossible dream!). Thus, for the project as a whole, the requirements must be prioritised in terms of what is essential, and what could be managed without (at least for a while). The acronym MoSCoW has become the watchword for this prioritisation. This stands for:

● **Must have** for requirements that are fundamental to the system. Without them the system will be unworkable and useless. The Must Haves define the **minimum usable subset**. A DSDM project guarantees to satisfy all the minimum usable subset.

● **Should have** for important requirements for which there is a work-around in the short term and which would normally be classed as mandatory in less time-constrained development, but the system will be useful and usable without them.

- **Could have** for requirements that can more easily be left out of the increment under development.

- **Want to have but Won't have this time round** for those valuable requirements that can wait till later development takes place.

The MoSCoW classification provides the basis on which decisions are made about what the project team will do over the whole project and during any timebox within the project.

As new requirements arise or as existing requirements are defined in more detail, the decision must be made as to how critical they are to the success of the current work using the MoSCoW rules. All priorities should be reviewed throughout the project to ensure that they are still valid.

It is essential that not everything to be achieved within a project or a timebox is mandatory. It is the lower level requirements that enable the teams to deliver on time by dropping out lower priority requirements when problems arise.

5   Project Management Requirements for Timeboxing

To achieve the benefits of timeboxing, the following aspects of project management and control need particular attention and skilful handling:

- **Planning**: this is the vital. Activities within the timebox must be carefully and accurately (as far as possible) planned before the timebox begins. There will be little scope for tuning the activities subsequently.

- **Realistic objectives**: the amount to be achieved, from both the IT and user perspective, must be clearly understood, and must be realistic within the time limit.

- **Realistic scope**: it is vital that the scope of the product is clearly defined and agreed by all parties <u>before</u> the work commences. Scope drift cannot be accommodated in this context.

- **Effective management**: the manager of a timeboxed project must keep very tight control over use of time and resources. It will also be necessary to motivate IT staff, to communicate clearly the scope and objectives to all staff, and to ensure that the need for contributions from different quarters does not result in delay.

- **Monitoring**: the progress of the project must be continuously monitored, for two purposes:

- as work progresses, the project leader must ensure that the team continually identifies the aspects of greatest relevance to the business, and that the project continually focuses on those aspects;

- any slippage must be identified immediately, and the appropriate corrective action taken.

● **Clear definition of responsibilities**: it would be inappropriate to waste time by duplicating effort, or to discover at the end of the timebox that key tasks had been overlooked.

● **Clear definition of deliverables**: the nature and content of the deliverables must be established before starting the timebox.

● **Commitment**: all individuals involved in the timebox must be motivated, and to a great extent must be able to work on their own initiative, contributing to the objectives of the whole project.

● **Availability**: one of the major planning functions of the project leader is to determine when the involvement of users and other contributors will be needed. It is vital that such involvement is agreed, and that the relevant people are available at the relevant time. Any slippage here will seriously endanger the goals of the timebox.

6   Recommended Approach to Timeboxing

● identify management role;

● agree scope and objectives of timebox activity;

● identify timebox participants;

● plan timebox activities;

● negotiate and agree availability of participants;

● allocate personal responsibilities and objectives;

● ensure continuing support;

● monitor relevance of work;

● monitor slippage;

● review progress weekly;

● review project achievement at end of timebox.

6.1 Identify management role

Appoint suitable project leader, who has a full understanding of the nature of timeboxing. Ensure that reporting structures are clear, and their requirements understood. Ensure that the project leader has appropriate authority and support to drive the project.

6.2 Agree scope and objectives of timebox activity

The project leader should evaluate the initial outline of the scope of the project, and ensure that it is feasible within the constraints of a timebox. The size of the timebox should be estimated and negotiated in the light of the scope. If necessary, renegotiate the scope. What the timebox will provide should be defined by the project leader, and agreed by users and IT management.

6.3 Identify timebox participants

It is vital that at least one user with adequate understanding of the business area is always available to the project, as part of the project team.

It is important that all project team members are adequately skilled and experienced to be able to work without a great deal of supervision.

6.4 Plan timebox activities

The activities to be performed in the timebox are left to the team to decide in order to produce the agreed product. However the team must plan the use of resources with as much precision as possible, especially with regard to the effort allocated to each task, and the individuals who will have responsibility for each task. Iteration is allowed within a timebox but must be planned for.

6.5 Negotiate and agree availability of participants

Input needed for parties other than core team members is likely to be identified. It is essential that recipients of requests for input regard them as being of high priority, otherwise delays will ensue. If possible, draw up a clear contract for the use of other parties.

6.6 Allocate personal responsibilities and objectives

Inform all project team members of their responsibilities and objectives. Adjust the plan if necessary. Provide any training needed to ensure that all responsibilities can be reliably fulfilled.

6.7 Ensure continuing support

As work progresses, specific requirements for information, advice, technical support etc. will be identified. It is the project leader's role to smooth the way for the project, and to ensure that any such requirements are recognised and satisfied as rapidly as possible.

6.8 Monitor relevance of work

Effort must be focused on the critical areas of the business, as identified by the users. The view of criticality may change during the project; it is the responsibility of the project leader to monitor the relevance of the work, and adjust if necessary.

6.9 Monitor slippage

The original plan must be very carefully produced, but will still be subject to delays, the reasons for which may or may not be outside the control of the project. As the plans begin to slip, the reasons for slippage must be identified and compensating action decided on. Usually this will mean rescheduling parts of the work or, as a last resort, de-scoping the project (any exclusions from scope should be agreed with the users). Extending the deadline of the timebox is not an option, as this tends to defeat the object of timeboxing.

6.10 Review progress weekly

Hold formal reviews of progress at weekly intervals to ensure the project remains on course. These reviews should be as flexible and unobtrusive as possible, to avoid impinging on getting on with the job. It should not be regarded as a substitute for monitoring key areas on a day-to-day basis; both are essential.

6.11 Review project achievement at end of timebox

Hold a formal review of the results of the timebox as soon as the final deadline is reached. The review should be scheduled in the original plans. Attendees should include the timebox participants and the project sponsor. Formally present the products of the timebox, and cover the following issues:

● **The acceptability of deliverables** from the timebox. Possible outcomes:

  • the work done is appropriate and suitable to progress with;

  • the products are not yet at a suitable level of completeness, and another iteration of a timebox is appropriate;

  • the timebox has not delivered sufficient of value, and the approach, along with some or all of the deliverables, should be abandoned for this project.

● **Conduct of project**: lessons to be learned, as the result either of failures or successes.

● **Subsequent action**: identify the ways in which the results of the timebox should be progressed.

6.12   How large should the timebox be?

A timebox should be in the range of 2 to 6 weeks. Of course, within the timebox the team will set goals of what has to be achieved by particular times, so that progress can be monitored.

The timebox (like DSDM in general) works best when the development team is supported by tools that enable speedy delivery of products, be they documents or software. The team must not be hindered by the absence of technology (tools) which will allow evolutionary prototyping.

Estimating

7.   Estimating

The underlying purpose of estimating is the same regardless of whether the project is to use a traditional approach or DSDM: to determine the resources required and therefore the cost of development for a particular system.

7.1   What's different about estimating in DSDM?

Specifically, in DSDM, it is stated that the cost associated with bringing the team 'up to speed' is outside DSDM since the team should be highly skilled in the development environment (the use of tools and techniques etc). The estimate is therefore one of *team development effort for the project **not** the project and skill acquisition*. However what is specifically included in comparison to other methods is the user effort, since users are team members not simply information providers.

DSDM does not allow contingency to be built into the estimates and relies upon very tight timescales with frequent delivery of products to focus the team's effort.

By the very nature of the DSDM approach, estimating is more accurately carried out using estimating techniques which are based upon high level outline business functions. This is entirely consistent with the DSDM focus upon Products rather than Activities.

7.2   When to estimate and who does it

Since DSDM is based on frequent delivery of products it is recommended that estimates are adjusted at the start of each timebox. There are two points where estimates are mandatory:

- at the end of Feasibility Study – here the purpose is to assess the practicality of the project in terms of cost within a DSDM framework and to develop an Outline Plan;

● at the end of Business Study – since the project will now have been scoped, functionality to be included and an outline prototyping plan will allow refinement of the initial estimate. The definition of the project and the team size will permit definition of timebox lengths.

Quite simply, the team does the estimating for the simple reason that if they agree the tight timescales then they are more likely to achieve those than if they had the timescales thrust upon them.

7.3 The estimating process

The estimating process has a number of distinct steps but is nevertheless an iterative process. The steps are:

● estimate the effort required;

● adjust the effort for environmental factors;

● identify the products and the dependencies between them;

● schedule the product deliveries and allocate resource;

● adjust the schedule in the light of known constraints (time for example!).

There are two classes of approach to estimating, **top down** and **bottom up**:

● **top down**: this begins with a view of the overall project and attempts to classify the whole project in a number of ways eg cost, complexity. The major components of the project can then be estimated using ratios. These ratios may be industry standard ratios or may be ratios tuned to the individual development environment and development type;

● **bottom up**: this begins by breaking the project down into smaller components which can be reliably estimated. These low level estimates are added together to give estimates for larger parts of the project until eventually the whole project estimate has been derived.

Use of both classes of estimating approach allows the team to calibrate the estimates for a particular type/size of project within a specific development environment. This should provide more accurate estimates of project resource costs.

7.3.1 The approaches to estimating

The discussion which follows is not specifically DSDM but provides a collection of approaches for illustration leading to detailed discussion of one approach, Function Point Analysis, which is well documented and well suited to DSDM.

The following approaches, whilst not exhaustive, illustrates the variety which is available:

- **Task based approach**: this is based upon tasks or activities which will be performed during the project. It is relevant where the method to be used in the project is strongly task-oriented. Task based estimating is easier where initial estimates are required;

- **Product based approach**: product deliverables are the basic unit for estimating and it is particularly appropriate where the method is strongly orientated toward product definition;

- **Algorithmic approach**: the algorithmic approach is used to eliminate the subjective judgements that must be made in estimating. It uses historical data on past projects (industry standard or organisation specific) which have been adjusted for the specific project environment. Formulae are used to calculate the estimates for the project;

- **Non-algorithmic approach**: this covers a whole raft of ploys for estimating from a largely intuitive approach through to a disciplined method. The more that it draws upon historical data, the more accurate the estimate is likely to be;

- **Analogy**: this is the experience route to an estimate. If an individual has performed a particular task before then they will be better placed to estimate a similar future task. Expert tools for estimating will capture this information for re-use. Obviously analogy will rely upon an accurate comparison between the project and other historical projects, the accuracy of the estimate which is produced being dependent upon the 'goodness of fit'. For this reason some adjustment may be required to compensate for any differences. Analogy is particularly appropriate in the early stages of the project where only the broad characteristics of the project are known with very little detail;

- **Expert judgement**: here the knowledge and expertise of individuals is used to obtain estimates based on previous experience. Experienced project managers who have worked on similar projects in the past may provide these estimates. Such estimates give a top down approach to estimating the whole project. The approach may also be implemented using experts in particular activities to provide estimates on areas of the project, their estimates being combined to estimate the whole project;

- **Standard ratios**: standard percentage ratios for the various stages of a project are applied. Once a firm estimate has been made upon an early stage the ratios can then be applied to provide an estimate for future stages and the project as a whole;

● **Function Point analysis**: this is a top down algorithmic approach which uses some known key features of the new system to derive a Function Point Index (FPI) for it, weighted for the technical complexity of the project. The FPI is then applied against productivity figures to derive an estimate.

7.4 Function Point Analysis (Mk II)

Function Point Analysis (FPA) was developed for use on transaction orientated business application systems and it addresses human resource aspects of system development in cash or work hours terms.

It provides a measure of the system which is as far as possible, independent of the language and other technical features of the design and its implementation.

FPA requires the following pre-requisites:

● a general understanding of the system;

● a high level entity model;

● identification of the transactions for the new system.

The method for FPA is as follows:

7.4.1 Calculate the system size as unadjusted function points

The key features of the system which are needed at this stage are:

● number of inputs;

● number of primary entity types referenced;

● number of outputs.

....where inputs and outputs are usually counted from a user view. **NOTE:** Batch and On-line parts of the system should be sized separately

The total unadjusted function points (UFP) are calculated using three weighting values for each of these three key features:

W_I – weighting for inputs;

W_E – weighting for entity types referenced;

W_O – weighting for outputs.

These weightings are calibrated by the organisation for their particular development environment. Where such calibration is not available (new environment perhaps) industry standard average values are available:

$$W_I = 0.58;$$

$$W_E = 1.66;$$

$$W_O = 0.26.$$

The unadjusted function points are calculated according to:

UFP = I + E + O where

I = No. of Inputs x W_I

E = No. of primary entity types referenced x W_E

O = No. of Outputs x W_O

7.4.2 Make a technical complexity adjustment to the UFP to derive Adjusted Function Points

A number of components contribute to the functional complexity of a system and these are listed below:

C1	Data Communications
C2	Distributed Functions
C3	Performance
C4	Heavily used configuration
C5	Transaction rate
C6	On-line data entry
C7	End-user efficiency
C8	On-line update
C9	Complex processing
C10	re-usability
C11	Installation ease
C12	Operational ease
C13	Multiple sites
C14	Facilitate change
C15	Interfaces
C16	Security, Privacy
C17	User training
C18	Third party use
C19	Documentation
C20	(client defined)

For each of these factors a mark is awarded for "degree of influence" according to the following scale:

0 = Not present or no influence

1 = Insignificant influence

2 = Moderate influence

3 = Average influence

4 = Significant influence

5 = Strong influence throughout

The marks are added together to give the "Total Degrees of Influence"

The Technical Complexity Adjustment (TCA) is then calculated as:

$$TCA = 0.65 + [C \times (Total\ Degrees\ of\ Influence)]$$

where C is obtained from calibration or the industry standard value of 0.005 is used.

To derive the estimated size of the system (ESIZE) in adjusted function points the Unadjusted Function points are multiplied by the Technical Complexity Adjustment (TCA):

$$ESIZE = UFP \times TCA$$

7.4.3 Compare to the following table of typical function point achievements per person

By comparison with the following table and knowing the number of people involved with the project an estimate of time to complete the project can be arrived at.

I.S System Development – Typical Achievements per person		
Project	Function Points/month	Equivalent of lines of COBOL/day
Large U.S. Government	2	10
Traditional COBOL	8	40
3GL inc productivity aids	13	65
Well managed 4GL/CASE	35	175
Reasonable RAD	100	500
Best RAD	200	1000

(James Martin)

6.4.4 Complete Function Point Analysis

The previous step in 6.4.3 is a simplified approach to FPA and the reader is referred to the work of Symons in development of FPA Mk2 which is extremely comprehensively detailed in:

Estimating with Mk II Function Point Analysis which is a text in the Information Systems Engineering Library CCTA 1992 ISBN 0 11 330578 8

This reference details other formulae which can be used to determine Productivity, Effort, Delivery rate and Time all of which would be calibrated for the particular development environment.

7.5 Pitfalls of estimating

The subjectivity of various aspects of estimating procedures depend on the evaluation of the estimator e.g. complexity weightings discussed above. Poor calibration of the model for estimating can also make estimating a less than precise activity although calibration would become more accurate with increased application of the method. Even if the estimates are not as accurate as they could be, use of the chosen estimating method upon alternative technical solutions will allow comparison of those solutions.

One final salutary warning – Estimates have a tendency to become self-fulfilling since the estimate is used to define the project budget with the consequence that the project is adjusted to meet the budgetary figure!

Notes

Timeboxing and Estimating

© TCC   DSDMP/5/1

© TCC   DSDMP/5/2

Meeting a Deadline

*"Creative people in many walks of life have a deadline.
A magazine writer, television producer or seminar developer
creates material for a certain date.*

*Whatever else happens,
they must not fail to meet the deadline."*

James Martin 1991

© TCC   DSDMP/5/3

Notes

Timeboxing

- **What is a Timebox?**

- **Key characteristics**

- **Project management requirements**

- **Recommended approach**

© TCC

DSDMP/5/4

What is a Timebox?

| Jan | Feb | Mar | Apr | May |

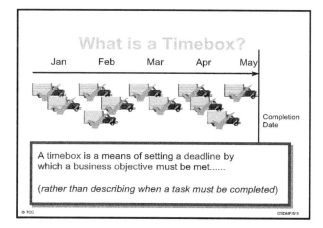

Completion Date

A timebox is a means of setting a deadline by which a business objective must be met......

(rather than describing when a task must be completed)

© TCC

DSDMP/5/5

Key characteristics of timeboxing

- **Time available dictates work done**

- **Review at deadline**

- **Reaffirm scope**

- **Prevent "drift"**

© TCC

DSDMP/5/6

Notes

Prioritisation

Must have
o
Should have
Could have
o
Would like but Won't have

© TCC — DSDMP/5/7

Timeboxing Requirements

- Planning
- Realistic objectives
- Realistic scope
- Effective management
- Monitoring

- •Clear responsibilities
- • Clear deliverables
- • Commitment
- • Available resources

© TCC — DSDMP/5/8

Timeboxing

Set Realistic Objectives!

Timebox ≠ Sweatbox!

© TCC — DSDMP/5/9

Notes

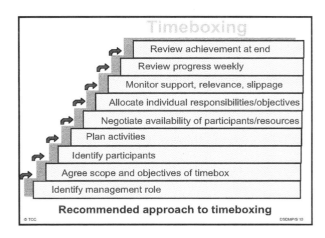

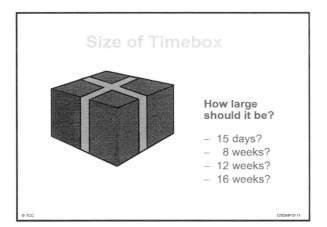

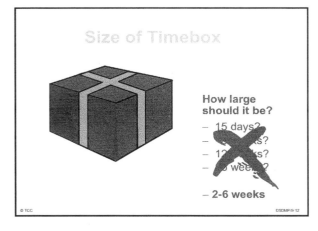

Notes

Timeboxing - Risks & Benefits

Benefits
- Prevents drift
- Ensures delivery in business "Window of Opportunity"

Risks
- Loss of functionality
- Failure to meet all objectives

© TCC   DSDMP/5/13

Planning Timeboxes

Plans:

- **Outline Plan** is produced by Feasibility Study

- **Outline Prototyping Plan** is produced by Business Study

- **Timebox Plan** to monitor progress throughout DSDM

© TCC   DSDMP/5/14

Timeboxing Summary

A Timebox:

forms a deadline for a business objective to be met

consists of an agreed scope and clear business objective

is typically two weeks (certainly no more than six)

will not be overrun - the deliverable may be de-scoped

contains activities defined by team members

© TCC   DSDMP/5/15

Notes

Estimating in DSDM

Estimating in DSDM:
- when is it done?

- who does it?

- what techniques are appropriate?

© TCC   DSDMP/5/16

Estimating in DSDM

Estimating in DSDM:
- when is it done?
    - feasibility study
    - business study
    - review at start of each timebox with adjustment of functionality if necessary (not size of timebox)
- who does it?
    - the DSDM team so that the entire team accepts the tight timescales
- what techniques are appropriate?
    - those techniques which operate on high level information eg Function Point Analysis
    - use of historical data (metrics of previous projects)

© TCC   DSDMP/5/17

The Estimating Process

There are a number of distinct steps:

- estimate the effort required

- adjust the effort for environmental factors

- identify the products and their inter-dependencies

- schedule the product deliveries and allocate resource

- adjust the schedule in the light of known constraints

© TCC   DSDMP/5/18

Notes

The Estimating Approaches

Approaches may be top-down or bottom up and include:

    task based
    product based
    algorithmic
    non-algorithmic
    analogy
    expert judgement
    standard ratios
    function point analysis

USE MORE THAN ONE APPROACH!

© TCC   DSDMP/5/19

FUNCTION POINT ANALYSIS Mk II

SYSTEM SIZE = **UNADJUSTED FUNCTION Pts** $(I \times W_I)+(E \times W_E)+(O \times W_O)$

+

TECHNICAL COMPLEXITY ADJ. $0.65 + (C \times \text{Complexity comp})$

WHERE:

Size of task:	Weightings related to required development effort:	Technical Complexity:
No. of Inputs = I No. of Entities Ref = E No. of Outputs = O	Weighting for input = W_I [0.58] Weighting for entities = W_E [1.66] Weighting for output = W_O [0.26] [Industry Standard values]	Calibration factor [0.005] 0.65 (constant)

© TCC   DSDMP/5/20

FUNCTION POINT ANALYSIS Mk II

Complexity Components:

C1	Data Communications	C11	Installation ease
C2	Distributed Functions	C12	Operational ease
C3	Performance	C13	Multiple sites
C4	Heavily used configuration	C14	Facilitate change
C5	Transaction rate	C15	Interfaces
C6	On-line data entry	C16	Security, Privacy
C7	End-user efficiency	C17	User training
C8	On-line update	C18	Third party use
C9	Complex processing	C19	Documentation
C10	re-usability	C20	(client defined)

SCALE: 0 = Not present or no influence   3 = Average influence
            1 = Insignificant influence   4 = Significant influence
            2 = Moderate influence   5 = Strong influence throughout

© TCC   DSDMP/5/21

Notes

FUNCTION POINT ACHIEVEMENT

I.S System Development - Typical Achievements per person		
Project	Function Points/month	Equivalent of lines of COBOL/day
Large U.S. Government	2	10
Traditional COBOL	8	40
3GL inc productivity aids	13	65
Well managed 4GL/CASE	35	175
Reasonable RAD	100	500
Best RAD	200	1000

James Martin 1990

© TCC

DSDMP/5/22

PROBLEMS WITH ESTIMATING

subjectivity of various aspects eg complexity weightings

insufficient experience/ previous history of developments with the development environment

estimates are self-fulfilling - project adjusted to fit budget

note: whilst estimates may not be as accurate initially
they can be a useful means for comparing different
technical approaches

© TCC

DSDMP/5/23

DSDM
Timeboxing and Estimating

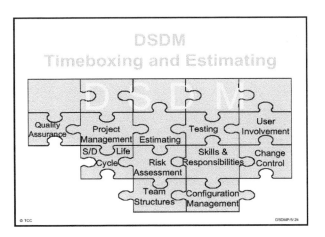

© TCC

DSDMP/5/24

Session 6
DSDM Products and Modelling Techniques

1 DSDM Products

DSDM lists product descriptions for each of the products defined within the DSDM Development Process Framework. The description defines a purpose for the product and a set of questions which can be asked to ensure that the purpose has been met. It also defines appropriate accepters of the product and the DSDM phase to which it relates. DSDM gives no details about how the products are built or what they should look like so that the product descriptions can be applied to all possible environments in which DSDM may be used.

2 The DSDM Products and Phases

The table below summarises the products and the phases to which they relate. Full details of each product are then given.

DSDM Phase	Products
Feasibility Study	**Feasibility Report**, possibly supported by a **Feasibility Prototype, an Outline Plan**
Business Study	**Business Area Definition** (including **Prioritised Requirements List**)
	System Architecture Definition
	Outline Prototyping Plan
Functional Model Iteration	**Functional Model** (including **Functional Prototypes** and a **Non-functional Requirements List**), together with supporting **Functional Model Review Records** and/or test records
	Implementation Strategy (including the strategy for data take-on, if appropriate)
	Development Risk Analysis Report
Design and Build Iteration	**Design Prototypes** (intermediate products), complete with supporting **Design Prototype Review records**
	Tested System, together with supporting **Test Records**
Implementation	**User Documentation**, showing how the computer system is to be used, together with identification of any supporting procedures which may be necessary
	Delivered System, together with supporting build, delivery and acceptance records
	Trained User Population (including operators and support staff)
	Project Review Document

The product descriptions are generic and should be refined for the specific business and development environments of each organisation using DSDM. This refinement can be achieved incrementally as experience in using DSDM grows. Caution should be used in developing the product descriptions. They should not be made so prescriptive that the flexibility that has been built into DSDM is lost through unnecessary bureaucracy. It should also be noted that many of the products, although generated in a particular stage of the life cycle, would need to be maintained during later stages.

2.1   Product descriptions

The numbering of the product descriptions indicates whether or not the products are "stand-alone" or a package of products. For instance, the Business Area Definition is numbered PD.3 which shows that it is complete in itself. The Prioritised Requirements List is numbered PD.3a to show that it is part of the Business Area Definition, but important enough to be treated as a separate product.

PD.1   Feasibility Report

Completed in: Feasibility Study
Suggested accepter: Visionary

Purpose

- To outline the problem to be addressed by the new system.

- To define the scope of the project or set of projects.

- To give a preliminary indication of any areas within the scope which may be desirable but not essential.

- To state, at least in outline, the Business Case for the project(s) – including where possible expected costs, benefits, assumptions and risks (whether quantifiable or not).

- To indicate what alternative solutions have been or could be considered.

- To define the major products to be delivered by the project.

- To report on the suitability of DSDM for use on the project, which may vary for each solution.

- To document the objectives of the project including process performance criteria.

- To document high-level technical and business constraints, e.g. timescale, hardware and software platforms.

● To identify whether the system may be safety-related or if there may be any product liability issues.

● To describe at a high level the business processes and data that are expected to be automated.

● To identify at a high level the interfaces necessary to existing data and applications.

● To identify which business processes and/or systems (whether automated or not) might be impacted by the new system and which might need to change in order to accommodate it.

● To define the expected life of the computer system and hence the requirements for maintainability as defined in Section 11.3.

Quality Criteria

1. Is the problem definition in line with the needs of senior user management?

2. Is the scope of the project sufficiently clear for it to be refined within the Business Study?

3. Are the business objectives to be met by the development clearly defined?

4. Is the solution to the problem, as laid out in the major products to be delivered and in the objectives of the project, feasible in both technical and business terms?

5. Is the case for using DSDM sound, i.e. does the application meet the criteria for using DSDM as laid out in the DSDM Manual?

6. Does management accept what has been included and excluded from the scope?

7. Are all associated systems and their interfaces identified? Is any impact on those systems acceptable?

PD.1a Feasibility Prototype

Completed in: Feasibility Study
Suggested accepters: Visionary, Technical Co-ordinator

Purpose

● To support the Feasibility Report in its findings.

● To provide a visualisation of the possible new computer system.

Quality Criteria

1. Does the prototype add value to the findings of the Feasibility Report?

2. If the prototype is automated, does it assist in the assessment of the suitability of DSDM to the application and development environment?

PD.2   Outline Plan

Completed in: Feasibility Study
Suggested accepters: Executive Sponsor, Visionary, Technical Co-ordinator

Purpose

- To provide management with a view of the financial and resource implications (both developer and user) of the proposed project.

- To provide a basis for agreement of timescales for the proposed development activities.

- To define the acceptance criteria for the proposed deliverables, e.g. the system will conform to all agreed requirements.

- To ensure that management are aware of the need for the development team (including users) to be empowered.

- To identify any particular facilities which the development team(s) will require (e.g. clean rooms, co-location).

- To define the required tailoring of the DSDM approach for this project.

- To confirm the approaches to configuration management, change control, testing and risk management.

- To identify any issues surrounding the implementation of the system, in particular aspects such as data take-on and user handover.

- To identify the required project standards and guidelines, e.g. for coding and for the style of the user interface, and to identify which of them already exist in a suitable form.

Quality Criteria

1. Are the estimates for effort realistic in the light of the details within the Feasibility Report?

2. Are the estimated timescales consistent with the business needs of the project? Conversely, have the business needs been addressed in terms of what is delivered and when?

3. Is user management able to commit the level of resources required of each type of user at the times stated in the project plan?

4. Is development management able to commit the level and type of resources required to meet the Outline Plan timescales?

5. Are the approaches to configuration management, change control and testing in line with existing procedures and within guidelines for DSDM?

6. Will all necessary equipment and facilities be available as required?

7. Is it clear what the criteria for acceptance are and are they rigorous enough to define the quality of deliverables while allowing the requirements to flex during development?

8. Are all the required standards and guidelines identified and available; for any which are not yet available, is sufficient resource allowed in the plan for their development or procurement?

PD.3   Business Area Definition

Completed in: Business Study
Suggested accepters: Visionary, Ambassador User(s), Project Manager

Purpose

●   To identify the business needs that should be supported by the proposed computer system.

●   To refine the Outline Business Case (documented in the Feasibility Report) to include benefits, risks, costs and impact analyses.

●   To outline the information requirements of the business processes that will be supported.

●   To identify the classes of users impacted by the development and introduction of the proposed system.

●   To identify the business processes and business scenarios that need to change.

●   To clarify all interfaces with other systems (human or automated).

●   To verify that the proposed system is still amenable to development using DSDM (tailored as necessary).

Quality Criteria

1. Are the business context, business process and business objectives defined and agreed?

2. Have all the currently identified requirements been prioritised (including non-functional requirements)?

3. Have all the priorities been assigned in collaboration with the users?

4. Have high-level acceptance criteria for the Delivered System been defined?

5. Are the business areas clearly documented, including high-level information needs that are affected by the system?

6. Is the envisaged boundary of the proposed new system realistic in the timescales?

7. Are all classes of users affected by the new system identified?

8. Are the information and processing requirements of the proposed system defined at least in outline?

9. Is it still clear that the business needs are being addressed by the proposed new system?

10. Is the person responsible for each business process identified? Can they commit the necessary resources and time?

11. Are all major business events identified?

PD.3a   Prioritised Requirements List

Purpose

● To provide the Functional Model Iteration with a prioritised list of requirements (both functional and non-functional) for investigation.

● To identify the minimum usable subset of functionality that will support the business. (This subset is guaranteed to be delivered.)

Quality Criteria

1. Have all the currently identified requirements been prioritised?

2. Have all the priorities been assigned in collaboration with the users?

3. If the development is in one project, does user management accept the possibility that low solutions to low priority requirements may not be delivered (at least initially)?

4. If the development is a set of projects, does user management the possibility that solutions to low priority requirements may not be delivered until a later?

PD.4   System Architecture Definition

Completed in: Business Study
Suggested accepters: Technical Co-ordinator, Project Manager,
                         Operations Co-ordinator

Purpose

- To provide a common understanding of the technical architectures to be used during development and implementation.

- To describe the target platform and (if different) the development platform.

- To give an outline description of the software architecture (i.e. the major software objects or components – both process and data – and their interactions).

Quality Criteria

1. Is the architecture appropriate for the requirements?

2. Have the risks in the proposed architecture been properly considered – in particular, are all components of the proposed architecture available and mutually compatible?

3. Will migration from the development platform to the target platform be able to occur easily? If not, are all foreseeable problems identified?

4. Is the outline software architecture sufficiently well defined to give developers a high-level view of the proposed computer system?

5. Is the architecture defined at an appropriate level, so that it will not be too vulnerable to change as the project progresses?

6. Has advantage been taken of any opportunities for reuse of existing components?

7. Can the architecture be expected to cope with performance, capacity and resilience requirements?

PD.5   Outline Prototyping Plan

Completed in: Business Study
Suggested accepters: Executive Sponsor, Visionary, Technical Co-ordinator

Purpose

- To refine the Outline Plan for the Functional Model Iteration and Design and Build Iteration.

- To provide the business analysts and designers with a strategy for development.

- To define the categories of prototypes which will be developed and when.

- To prioritise prototyping activities.

- To define the mechanisms for deciding when a particular prototyping activity should terminate.

- To identify individuals who will take on the various roles and responsibilities on forthcoming phases of the project.

- To identify which items are to be subject to configuration management and to outline how configuration control is to be applied.

- To define the approach to be taken to testing: what types of tests are to be run, how they are to be specified and recorded.

Quality Criteria

1. Are the timescales consistent with the business objectives in the Feasibility Report and the Business Area Definition?

2. Does the order of activities within the prototyping plan reflect the list of prioritised requirements?

3. Does the plan reflect the need to address areas of risk at appropriate times?

4. Are all affected classes of users identified in the prototyping plan?

5. Is the proposed user effort consistent with the needs of both the existing business processes and the development?

6. Will the necessary effort (from all personnel) be available when required?

7. Is the selection of the categories of prototypes feasible within the expected development environment?

8. Are the configuration items appropriate to the functionality in the Business Area Definition and to the deliverables in the Outline Plan?

9. Is the method of configuration management appropriate to the environment?

10. Are the proposed extent, depth and formality of testing appropriate?

PD.6   Functional Model

Completed in: Functional Model Iteration
Suggested accepters: Visionary, Ambassador User(s), Advisor User(s),
Technical Co-ordinator

Purpose

- To provide a cohesive demonstration of the functionality and data requirements to be met, including all currently known constraints.

- To demonstrate the feasibility of achieving the non-functional requirements.

Quality Criteria

1. Does the Functional Model match the users' needs as elicited during discussions and prototyping sessions?

2. Is it within the scope of the development as defined in the Business Area Definition?

3. Are all parts of the Functional Model mutually consistent?

4. Does the model contain the minimum usable subset?

5. Are all essential aspects of integrity and security contained within the Functional Model?

6. Are the requirements for system administration visible?

7. Are all static models (e.g. data models) consistent with the Functional Prototype, and vice versa?

8. Does the model give confidence that the right levels of performance, capacity and maintainability will be achievable?

9. Is any necessary supporting documentation available and to an adequate standard?

PD.6a   Functional Prototype

Completed in: Functional Model Iteration
Suggested accepters: Visionary, Ambassador User(s)

Purpose

- To provide a first-cut system component that contains most of the functionality required to support the business processes. (It does not necessarily have to meet the non-functional requirements, though it should give confidence that such requirements will be achievable.)

- To enable users to comprehend the facilities which the system will provide.

- To enable users to understand easily to what events they will be expected to respond, so that they can operate the new computer system effectively.

- To provide a basis for agreement with users at all levels about the direction the project is taking.

Quality Criteria

1. Are any and all paper-based components of the Functional Prototype achievable in the development environment?

2. Are all important system interfaces apparent, at least in outline? Does their later implementation look feasible?

3. Are all essential business process requirements identifiable in the Functional Prototype? Where they are not, is supporting documentation available?

4. Are all essential data requirements identifiable in the Functional Prototype? Where they are not, is supporting documentation available?

5. Where non-functional requirements have been addressed by the Functional Prototype are they clearly demonstrated?

PD.6b   Non-functional Requirements List

Completed in: Functional Model Iteration
Suggested accepters: Ambassador User(s), Technical Co-ordinator

Purpose

- To refine and expand the non-functional requirements for use in the Design and Build Iteration (even if they have been satisfied in a Functional Prototype).

Quality Criteria

1. Are all the non-functional requirements sufficiently quantified?

2. Where non-functional requirements have been addressed by the Functional Prototype, are these noted as such in the list of non-functional requirements?

3. Have all areas identified in the high level constraints in the Feasibility Report been considered?

4. Is the set of non-functional requirements complete and consistent both within itself and with the rest of the Functional Model?

5. Do all the non-functional requirements add value to the business processes?

6. Are the non-functional requirements realistic and achievable?

PD.6c   Functional Model Review Records

Completed in: Functional Model Iteration
Suggested accepters: Project Manager, Quality Manager

Purpose

- To record the user feedback for all functional models and prototypes.

- To assist in planning and executing design activities.

- To highlight any areas which can be implemented in future development work.

- To assist any future development in avoiding any pitfalls similar to ones which may have arisen so far on this project.

Quality Criteria

1. Do the review records cover all Functional Prototypes?

2. Are all comments from users recorded to their satisfaction?

3. Has user management agreed any areas for which users have requested further development?

4. Where unresolved conflicts of user requirements have arisen are these highlighted for management and/or technical consideration?

5. Do the review records provide sufficient information to show where the prototypes currently fall short of expectations?

6. If there are areas that should be "frozen" as they are (e.g. some part of the user interface), do the review records highlight them?

PD.7   Implementation Strategy

Completed in: Functional Model Iteration
Suggested accepters: Technical Co-ordinator, Operations Co-ordinator

Purpose

● To refine the project plan for the later stages of the development.

● To define the costs and effort in more detail, enabling management to reassess the costs and benefits of the development.

Quality Criteria

1. Does the design and build timetable still fit in with business needs?

2. Do the cost and effort estimates (both developer and user) look realistic?

3. Are the necessary resources (both developer and user) available to meet this plan?

4. If relevant, are the procedures for handover to maintenance and support staff clear?

5. If relevant, have the requirements for data take-on and/or system cutover been adequately considered?

PD.8   Development Risk Analysis Report

Completed in: Functional Model Iteration
Suggested accepters: Executive Sponsor, Visionary, Ambassador User(s)

Purpose

● To assist management in deciding the future of the project.

● (Note: Risk analysis starts at the beginning of the project, but given the short time scales of DSDM projects to delivery of an increment, this is the latest point at which the development of risk avoidance or containment strategies are feasible. Risks that emerge from here on will probably be handled more reactively.)

Quality Criteria

1. Are all the factors potentially affecting the success of the project discussed?

2. Are risks sufficiently quantified for a decision to be made?

3. Does each risk have at least one countermeasure identified?

PD.9   Design Prototype

Completed in: Design and Build Iteration
Suggested accepters: Technical Co-ordinator, Ambassador User(s), Advisor
                         User(s)

Purpose

- To provide developers with assurance that a particular design strategy is feasible.

- To provide users (particularly senior users) with evidence that development is progressing in the right direction.

- To provide users with the opportunity to help improve the system through feedback to the developers.

Quality Criteria

1. Does the prototype satisfactorily address the intended issues?

2. Are all risks in progressing with the design clearly identified?

3. Does the design conform to all applicable user requirements?

4. Does the design conform to all applicable development standards and guidelines?

PD.9a   Design Prototyping Review Records

Completed in: Design and Build Iteration
Suggested accepters: Project Manager, Quality Manager

Purpose

- To record the user feedback for all Design Prototypes.

- To help steer future developments clear of any pitfalls that may have been encountered.

- To highlight, and plan for, any areas that should be implemented or tuned either during the build phase or which may be addressed following delivery of the system.

Quality Criteria

1. Do the review documents cover all Design Prototypes?

2. Are all comments from users and developers recorded to their satisfaction?

PD.10   Tested System

Completed in: Design and Build Iteration
Suggested accepters: Visionary, Ambassador User(s), Technical Co-ordinator,
                        Operations Co-ordinator

Purpose

● To provide a system that performs all agreed functionality and which meets all the agreed non-functional requirements. (Due to business timescale constraints, the Tested System might cover only an agreed subset of all the functional and non-functional requirements.)

● To provide a working system which can be placed safely in the users' environment.

● To provide support and maintenance staff with sufficient information to perform enhancements, support the users, perform system management tasks, etc.

Quality Criteria

1. Does the system satisfy all the user-defined acceptance criteria?

2. Are the developers satisfied that the system is sufficiently robust to be put into full operation?

3. Has the system been tested at an appropriate level, considering its intended use?

4. Is there evidence that all the essential requirements (functional and non-functional) have been tested and, where necessary, demonstrated to the users?

5. Have any and all safety-related and product liability aspects of the system been properly validated?

6. Has all functionality that is provided to support implementation been adequately tested (in particular, has account been taken of any need for data conversion/uploading software)?

7. Are all components of the Tested System traceable to the Functional Model?

8. Are all components rejected in the design review documents omitted from the Tested System?

9. Is the system documentation consistent with the software?

PD.10a Test Records

Completed in: Design and Build Iteration
Suggested accepters: Project Manager, Quality Manager

Purpose

- To show that tests have been performed in accordance with the test plan identified in the Outline Prototyping Plan.

Quality Criteria

1. Have tests been appropriately documented (for example does each test identify the requirements and business rules addressed by the test)?

2. If appropriate, have test specifications been reviewed?

3. Are records available to show that all required tests have been performed and that the user involvement in that testing is as required?

4. Have all problems noted during testing been properly identified and recorded?

5. Have regression tests been performed appropriately?

6. Do the Test Records contain sufficient detail to enable the tests to be run again in future?

PD.11   User Documentation

Completed in: Implementation
Suggested accepters: Ambassador User(s)

Purpose

- To describe to the users how to use the Delivered System.

Quality Criteria

1. Is user guidance available to users in an appropriate format (e.g. electronic documents, paper documents, and help facilities)?

2. Does it offer a complete and unambiguous step-by-step guide to using the Delivered System?

3. Does it cover all the functionality within the system as delivered?

4. Does it explain how the system interacts with other systems, manual or otherwise?

5. Where there are different classes of user, does it explain who should read what?

6. Is it easy to reference by business-based tasks?

7. Is it written in the language of the user population?

8. If required, does it offer step-by-step explanations of any manual procedures associated with the computer system?

9. Does it contain guidance on what to do when errors arise, for instance, whom to call and standard approaches to recovery and problem solving?

10. If it contains a tutorial, is this easy to follow? Has a new user tried it out?

PD.12 Trained User Population

Purpose

- To enable all users to use and operate the computer system and any new business processes effectively.

Quality Criteria

1. Do the trained users have sufficient knowledge and skill to manage and operate the system?

2. Have all relevant users received the necessary training?

3. If required, is any ongoing training material for future users available?

4. Is the User Documentation easily available to all users?

5. Has a strategy been devised to train future new members of the user population?

6. Has a strategy been devised to train existing users in future developments of the system?

PD.13 Delivered System

Completed in: Implementation
Suggested accepters: Executive Sponsor, Visionary, Ambassador User(s), Advisor User(s), Technical Co-ordinator, Operations Co-ordinator

Purpose

- To perform the functionality described in the Functional Model in accordance with all constraints defined in the non-functional requirements.

Quality Criteria

1. Have any changes made to the Tested System (see PD.10) been properly authorised, implemented and tested?

2. Does the system work as required in its target environment?

3. Does it appear to operate to the required service levels?

4. Are there any unforeseen problems in the system's placement in the target environment that remain unresolved?

5. Have all data loading and conversion activities been completed successfully?

6. Have all configuration items been properly archived?

7. Are all configuration items identified?

8. Is the correct version of each configuration item recorded?

9. Are all known outstanding problems recorded?

PD.14   Project Review Document

Completed in: Implementation
Suggested accepters: Executive Sponsor, Visionary, Ambassador User(s)

Purpose

● To assess the success of the development work.

● To enable decisions on future development work to be made.

● To decide what deliberate omissions could now be addressed.

Quality Criteria

1. Have all areas, which were omitted in this increment, been identified?

2. Is there sufficient information to enable management to decide whether or not to proceed with further development work?

3. Have all lessons learned during the increment been documented?

3   DSDM modelling techniques

3.1   Introduction to modelling techniques

Many Systems Analysis and Design methods exist which detail the modelling techniques, which are "best practice" in the engineering approach to building software. Such techniques should underpin a DSDM project, at an appropriate level, to ensure the integrity of the resulting software.

DSDM does not mandate specific techniques. Rather, it aims to identify and describe the various **perspectives** from which system modelling should be considered and the way the models relate to the DSDM products.

3.2   Definition of terminology

The following terms are used throughout this chapter:

- **Model:** an abstraction of some characteristic of the business or system, as seen from a particular viewpoint;

- **Modelling Technique:** a means by which a diagrammatic representation of a specific aspect of the system or business area is developed;

- **DSDM Product:** a collection of one or more models, plus other project information;

- **DSDM Tool:** computer assisted support for one or more techniques, including the building of the final computer system.

3.3   Issues when selecting techniques for DSDM

In trying to identify a set of candidate modelling techniques suitable for application to rapid development there are several issues that need to be borne in mind.

3.3.1   Rapid development

DSDM is concerned with the faster introduction of systems into operational use. Therefore any technique identified should not impose any undue bureaucratic overheads on the project. Many techniques can cause an unnecessary burden on the project; in particular when a project moves between differing phases, for example from requirements analysis to logical design.

Many techniques require a change in the way that the system is thought about in different development phases. This means that a smooth transfer from, say, analysis to design is often difficult. For DSDM, with its inherent iteration and incremental delivery, the techniques used must be easily understood by user and developer alike and provide the means by which the system can be developed in a series of refinements. It is important, however, that the chosen modelling techniques should be capable of representing sufficient detail to assist with the build process, as required.

3.3.2   Communication

One of the main sources of misunderstandings and errors being introduced into a system development is the lack of good communication between all parties involved in the development process. Each party has its own particular jargon, whether it is the users, the developers, the technical experts or the managers, which leads to difficult communications. Therefore any technique must help communications by prompting developers in asking the right questions and by providing users with a means of checking that the system being developed is what is required. The users should easily understand any technique, together with the resultant model produced, at least in outline.

3.3.3   Semantic gap

The semantic gap refers to the natural difference in the viewpoint taken on any system development between the end users and the system developers. Naturally the business concerns are with the business tasks and scenarios, and they will talk about the proposed computer system in these terms. On the other hand, the developers and implementers view the computer system from a more technical viewpoint. They view it in terms of specific applications, and in terms of databases, communications, computers and support packages.

These differing viewpoints have historically led to misunderstandings and the development of computer systems, which did not live up to the users' expectations. The DSDM team can bridge the semantic gap caused by these alternative languages by adopting a user-centred approach to computer system development and ensuring that, as much as possible, the system is viewed from the user/business perspective.

One approach that could be considered within a DSDM project is as follows:

● produce a sub-set of models, each reflecting the perspective of an individual class of user, focusing on their own limited view of the system. This can be used to support Functional Model Iteration;

● once each view has been refined via a series of functional prototypes, a consolidated model of the various individual views can be constructed to assist in achieving performance, reducing duplication, encouraging re-use and in subsequent maintenance. This more detailed technical view is best constructed during Design and Build Iteration, perhaps even after some early increments of functionality have actually been implemented.

A precursor to the first step, to reduce the risk of developing components which do not integrate together well, is to set screen/development standards in place and to identify an outline design architecture to act as a guiding framework for the user-focused developments. This does not need to be a lengthy process, and the key principles may be appropriate for development during a facilitated workshop.

3.4   DSDM modelling techniques

Modelling helps the DSDM development team gain a good understanding of the business and the developing system and can significantly aid communication. In understanding the problems, accurate models can be produced which reflect the realities of the business world. This understanding can be gained by considering the problem from different viewpoints.

A full picture of the business requirements and the developing system can be gained from modelling the perspectives: what, how, where, who, when and why.

These broadly follow a framework developed by John Zachman, and can be expanded as follows:

- **WHAT**   The entities and relationships within the business (data and relationships). This gives the **data view**.

- **HOW**   The functions and processes within the business, which transform input to outputs together with their interfaces (process and I/O). This gives the **processing view**.

- **WHERE**   The locations, at which the business operates, considered as nodes and lines (**locations** and network links).

- **WHO**   The people (agents) within the organisation and the work they do (users and tasks). This gives the **user interface view** and the interactions between who, what, how and when.

- **WHEN**   The events of importance to the business (time and scheduling). This is the **behavioural view**.

- **WHY**   The business view which models the **business objectives** and strategy from various perspectives and the ways of achieving them (rationale, ends and means).

The interactions between the above six perspectives may also require modelling. For example, the "why" perspective (rationale, ends and means) could usefully be mapped to the "how" perspective (process and I/O), allowing the business justification for each process to be confirmed.

3.4.1   Modelling from the perspective of a single user

Rather than model the entire business area at once in these terms, it may be more appropriate to model the aspects needed for the user to be able to carry out a **specific task**. This approach is more likely to achieve individual user buy-in. It will ensure that each user is able to focus on areas which are of most interest to themselves, and in which they have the most knowledge and experience to contribute.

The user-centred (task-based) view cuts across the above perspectives, providing the answer to all six questions for a specific user responding to a specific business event. Techniques that support the user-centred view will need to be supported by broader, IT-centred techniques and models to provide the detailed and integrated view of data, behaviour, and processing necessary to build the computer system.

In order to avoid duplication of identical components across users, care should be taken to consolidate the individual user views into a single model supporting the overall system. Once a model has been identified in this way it should be re-used as much as possible throughout the current and subsequent developments. It may be useful to consider maintaining a repository of the components of these models (either as items of data, process or interface or as integrated objects) in order to encourage a component-based approach to development. Tool support is strongly recommended to provide the means for achieving this.

3.4.2   Modelling and abstraction

Modelling usually incorporates some degree of **abstraction**, which involves omitting certain details from any particular model to allow clear focus on another particular aspect. Some models may be physical, incorporating aspects of *how, when, where, why, who, what*, and some logical, concentrating on just *what* (what data, what processes, what interactions between these).

For some complex systems, where the non-functional requirements of the system are considered to be a prime risk, additional models may have to be developed to model such characteristics as security or performance.

Within DSDM some models can be animated, in the form of various prototypes. Some tools can generate working prototypes from the models, and some will allow models to be extracted from the prototypes themselves. Ideally, tools should be capable of maintaining the models and prototypes in synchrony with each other.

3.4.3   Modelling the system from different perspectives

The various models can be viewed from the perspectives of different "agents" or roles at different points in the DSDM life-cycle.

DSDM Life-Cycle Phase	Agent (DSDM role)	View Description
Feasibility	Planner (Executive Sponsor/ Visionary)	This corresponds to an executive summary for the planner or investor and covers the "size and shape" of the system and cost/benefit analysis
Business Study	Owner (Ambassador User)	This depicts the business entities and processes and how they will interact, from the perspective of the owner, who will have to live and work with the system.
Functional Model Iteration	Designer (Developer)	This gives a detailed logical specification from the designer's perspective
Design and Build Iteration	Builder (Developer) (Technical Co-ordinator)	This gives a detailed physical specification from the perspective of the builder, who will physically construct the element. It incorporates the constraints of tools, technology and other resources,
Implementation	User (Ambassador/Advisor User)	This is the documentation and working components of the final system.

Examples of the types of modelling techniques that may be appropriate for each life-cycle phase are given in the Table shown overleaf. When consulting the table, it should be borne in mind that the Functional Model and Design and Build Iterations may overlap or even merge, depending on the tools used to build the system.

3.5 Using models for the DSDM products

Models used in software development can be grouped into two main categories:

- **Development Models**: those models which are produced and required during the development of the system;

- **Maintenance Models**: those models which are required by the maintainers of the computer system.

Therefore two categories of DSDM modelling techniques can be defined:

- **Core Techniques**: which produce key models of the system which will be required to develop and maintain the system;

- **Support Techniques**: which contain supporting information which is usually only required during the development phases.

Generally speaking, at a minimum the models produced by the Core Techniques should be included in all DSDM documentation.

3.6 Application development

The tables below summarise the DSDM products and suggest the models to be considered during each phase of DSDM. Many of the models listed fulfil exactly the same purpose as each other. It would not, in any project, be appropriate to attempt to develop them all. The techniques should be selected carefully to achieve the objectives stated for each phase, and to produce the set of products necessary to the project.

The decision as to which specific techniques are used to populate the table for a particular development is influenced by a number of factors including:

● type of system (e.g. traditional information system, internet/intranet development);

● development environment;

● skills/experience of the development team.

DSDM phase	DSDM products	Objectives of modelling (What, How, Where, Who, When, Why)	Examples of models	Examples of interactions which may be appropriate
Feasibility Study	Feasibility Report Feasibility Prototype Outline Plan	**Scope and Enterprise Model** • Key Business Data • Key Business Activities • Key business locations • Key People/ Users • Key Events • Business Vision/ Scope/ Objectives plus • Key Interfaces	**Core Models:** • Critical Success Factors • Context Diagram **Support Models:** • Rich Picture • Function Hierarchy • Network Architecture Plan • Workflow Diagram • Organisation Chart	• Entity/ Organisation • Entity/ Process • Process/ Location • Process/ Organisation • Major Event/ Location • Location/ Role • Objective/ Responsibility

DSDM phase	DSDM products	Objectives of modelling (What, How, Where, Who, When, Why)	Examples of models	Examples of interactions which may be appropriate
Business Study	Business Area Definition Outline Prototyping Plan System Architecture Definition	**Enterprise Model** **High-level System Model** • Business Functions Data/Relationships/ Rules • Business Events • Business Scenarios • Business Architecture • System Locations • System Users	**Core Models:** • Entity Relationship Model (high-level) • Business Process Model • High Level Data Flow Diagrams • Critical Success Factors • Business Object Model • Use Cases • Technical Architecture Model **Support Models:** • Function Dependencies • Business Scenarios • Task Models • Business Event Model	• Process/Entity • Process/ Location • Event Location • Person Role/ system role • CSF/Process • Task/Object
Functional Model Iteration	Functional Model Implementation Strategy Development Risk Analysis Report	**System Model** • Functional Prototypes • Requirements (functional and non-functional)	**Core models:** • Logical Data Model • Data Flow Diagrams • Use Cases • Screens/Menus • Object Model **Support Models:** • Process Dependencies • Scenario analysis • Object Interaction/Collaborati on Diagrams • User Conceptual Model • User Interface Object Model • Screen Navigation Design • Network Topology Model • System Events • System State Diagram • Object Dynamic Models	Process/Entity User role/Function

DSDM phase	DSDM products	Objectives of modelling (What, How, Where, Who, When, Why)	Examples of models	Examples of interactions which may be appropriate
Design and Build Iteration	Tested system meeting all the agreed functional and non-functional requirements Design prototypes	**Technology Model Components Model** Tested System: • Screens/ Menus/ Reports • System users and locations • Technology strategy	**Core models:** • Physical Data Model • Physical Process Model • Object Distribution Map • Network Topology Model • Code **Support models:** • Detailed User Process Models	• System role/user • System event/business event • Application/ object • Platform/ Application • User/ Application Data Structure/ Application • Data Structure/ Storage • Entity/Data Structure
Implemen-tation	User Documentati on Trained User Population Delivered System Project Review Document	**Functioning, Tested, Documented System** (including User Documentation/ Help Information	**Core models:** • Physical Components Structure • Help Information • User/ Operational Task Descriptions **Support Models:** • Physical Components Definition • Security Architecture	• Function/ Access Control • User/Function

3.7   User-centred development

The techniques selected to support DSDM should initially concentrate on modelling the computer system from a user's perspective. This approach has been called "User-Centred Development" (UCD), as the techniques are not only easily understood by the user but they also model concepts familiar to the user. UCD should contain not only the techniques to describe the internal processing and data aspects of the development, but also a set of techniques for the development of user interfaces, in respect of both requirements and constraints. User interface techniques are oriented both to the user and to more formal models, and include the following:

● **User Analysis** which provides insight into the range and responsibilities of the end-users of the proposed computer system and produces a catalogue of the various classes of users, their jobs, skills, access requirements, etc.;

● **Usability Analysis** which determines the characteristics of the proposed interface design which will satisfy the users' non-functional requirements;

- **Task Modelling** which models the various activities to be performed by the users of the system;

- **Task Scenario Definition** which identifies particular instances of task execution for any given system user;

- **User Conceptual Modelling (User Object Modelling)** which produces a model of the computer system from the user's perspective that is simply understood by the users of the system. An illustration of such a model is the typical map of the railway network or Metro, where the detail provided is just sufficient to allow journey-planning, without unnecessary technical details;

- **Graphical User Interface Design** which produces the interface for the user which provides support for the identified tasks, within the project constraints;

- **User Interface Prototyping** which provides an animated view of the proposed design of the user interface.

Finally, these initial user-centred models are refined further by the application of more formal IT-centred design techniques, such as **data, behaviour and process models**. These need to be cross-referenced to the user-centred views for consistency. Further refinements are performed on the formal models of the computer system, until the most detailed model of the system is developed, namely code itself. The choice of interface modelling techniques is not influenced by the approach taken to modelling the underlying functionality and data.

The above list of techniques is not meant to be exhaustive, but it provides a carefully selected range of techniques that could be applied on a DSDM project. Many other techniques can be used. Indeed the approach proposed within DSDM is to capitalise on existing knowledge and experiences within any user organisation. However, care should be taken to document only what is absolutely essential and only to the level of detail which enables understanding. The system should be documented in the code (or at the level at which it is generated). Longer, slower projects, without consistent user involvement, by their very nature tend to need more interim documentation than DSDM projects.

3.8   Selection of techniques

Selection of a technique set for use within a DSDM project can be made according to a number of criteria. There are various factors to be considered in building up the set to be delivered as part of the DSDM products defined above.

The basis on which techniques are selected for use within DSDM are generally:

- the level of overhead;

- do user and developer easily understand it?

- does it support process of serial refinement?

- do the models produced enhance communication?

- does the technique lie easily within the DSDM framework?

More specifically a technique must be evaluated against the following principles.

3.8.1   Software engineering discipline

System development can be quite prone to errors introduced for a number of reasons. To attempt to avoid errors an engineering approach to the problem has been incorporated within systems development methods. DSDM is no exception in this respect. The aim is to understand the application BEFORE development commences, to model the different views of the system through a series of essential models/prototypes and model the system in business terms.

3.8.2   Model building approach

By continuously developing and improving system models to describe the system, essential information is captured and non-essential information left out. Hence the complexity of the system is recorded in a way which allows the information to be managed and controlled.

3.8.3   Model refinement

As with many development methods DSDM requires techniques which will allow refinement of the models at both the logical and the physical level. The former describes the logical system irrespective of the technology whilst the latter describes the current physical system or the physical way that the new system will be implemented.

3.8.4   Communication aid

In common with other development methods, the techniques which are used should aid communication between team members as well as users and senior management. If communication is of a high quality the misunderstandings and ambiguous interpretations which foster system errors can be avoided.

3.8.5   Re-use

DSDM reduces the development time for a functional information system. One obvious way to do this is to re-use components that were developed for other systems. (re-invention of the wheel is to be avoided). Any technique which produces re-usable development components is therefore appropriate to use in DSDM.

3.8.6   Traceability

As stated previously DSDM operates by refinement of models/prototypes. To audit the trail of the refinement process it must be possible to trace the path both backward and forward from a particular version of the model. In this way traces between user requirements and system components can be used to ensure that all requirements have been met or moved outside the scope of the project. Either way what the fate of each requirement has been must be determinable. Another area where the trace is important is in testing where the requirement definition forms the basis against which acceptance tests can be performed on each requirement.

3.8.7   DSDM product support

DSDM is a product based approach and therefore the techniques selected must deliver something which is part of the DSDM product set.

3.8.8   Business focus

Since DSDM actively involves users and is concerned with business issues, the techniques should be directed towards tackling business problems. The technique should enable the business activities and rules of the business to be modelled.

3.8.9   User focus

The active involvement of users requires that any technique to be used should be easily understood by users and developers.

3.8.10   Prototyping

Prototype development is fundamental in DSDM and therefore if a technique promotes and supports the development of prototypes and animated models it should be considered appropriate for use within DSDM.

3.8.11   Non-functional requirements

Techniques for DSDM must support the non-functional requirements of the new system as well as the functional requirements. These non-functional requirements are:

- **Performance**: these required system values, such as response rates, capacity volumes and communication rates;

- **Interface**: these specify the hardware or software elements with which the system must interact or communicate;

- **Operational**: these specify how the system will run and communicate with the system users, including all user interface requirements;

- **Resource**: these specify the machine resource requirements, such as memory, disk capacity and processor power;

- **Documentation**: these specify the project-specific documentation requirements;

- **Security**: these specify security requirements against threats to confidentiality, integrity and availability;

- **Portability**: these detail the need for the system to be capable of installation onto other hardware/operating system platforms;

- **Reliability**: these specify the acceptable mean time between failures of the system, averaged over a significant period;

- **Maintainability**: these specify how easy it is to repair faults and adapt the software to new requirements;

- **Safety**: these specify the requirements to reduce the possibility of causing damage as a direct result of system failure.

3.8.12   Builds on existing knowledge

DSDM is not prescriptive about the techniques to be used and therefore it makes sense to capitalise on the investment in skills training already made by the organisation. The experience of the DSDM team in the techniques will also keep the development on target, an objective which would be compromised by uptake of new techniques (not recommended).

3.8.13   Method independence

Within an organisation some projects may be RAD (DSDM) projects whilst others follow some other development approach. Selecting the techniques for use within a DSDM project should not force any organisation to adopt a particular system development approach for all of its other projects. The choice will of course be influenced as described in the previous section.

3.8.14   Requirements management

Business requirements must be supported by DSDM techniques. Early in a DSDM project, prototyping serves to elicit user requirements, which can be fed back into the development process if appropriate. Later in the system design and build phase yet further requirements may emerge which it is not possible to include in this particular incremental development. Rather than lose these, it is helpful if the techniques can support capture of this information perhaps for inclusion in later enhancements to the system (as part of a later DSDM project)

3.9   Summary

The choice of possible techniques for use on a DSDM development is potentially large. Differing techniques will be applicable to differing phases of the project. In addition, some techniques will be more appropriate for use on one development project than another. DSDM must be sufficiently flexible to accommodate diversity and a wide range of interests.

Taking a user-centred approach, based on the tasks the user needs to perform (and the interface "objects" on which they need to perform these), is consistent with the development of computer systems using joint development teams, prototyping and workshops.

The user-centred approach results in the development of a set of models of the system that are:

- an effective means of communication between all parties;

- a way of capturing the essence of a problem, or design, such that it can be mapped into another form without loss of detail;

- a means of providing abstraction by hiding unwanted detail;

- a representation that provides insight into the business;

- an effective mechanism for scoping the business domain.

Notes

DSDM Products
and
Modelling Techniques

© TCC   DSDMP/6/1

Session Objectives

DSDM Products

Modelling Techniques

© TCC   DSDMP/6/2

DSDM Products

Feasibility Study   Feasibility Report, Feasibility Prototype (optional), Outline Plan

Business Study   Business Area Definition, System Architecture Definition
Prioritised Requirements List, Outline Prototyping Plan

Functional Model   Functional Model, Functional Prototypes,
Non-functional Requirements List, Functional Model Review Records
Development Risk Analysis Report, Implementation Strategy
Iteration

Design & Build   Design Prototypes, Design Prototype Review Records
Tested System, Test Records
Iteration

Implementation   User Documentation, Delivered System
Trained User Population, Project Review Document

© TCC   DSDMP/6/3

Notes

DSDM Product Descriptions

Each Product is defined in terms of:

- When produced

- Who could be responsible for accepting

- Its purpose

- Its quality (acceptance) criteria

© TCC   DSDMP/6/4

DSDM Product Descriptions

PD.3 Business Area Definition

Completed in	Business Study
Suggested Accepters	Visionary, Ambassador User(s), Project Manager

Purpose:
- to identify the business need that should be supported by the proposed system
- to refine the outline Business Case
- to outline the information requirements of the business processes to be supported
  ... etc ....

Quality Criteria:
1. Are the business context, business process and business objectives defined and agreed?
2. Have all the currently identified requirements been prioritised (including non-functional requirements)?
3. Have all the priorities been assigned in collaboration with the users?
  ... etc ....

Note: PD. 3 contains PD.3a

© TCC   DSDMP/6/5

Modelling Techniques within DSDM

© TCC   DSDMP/6/6

Notes

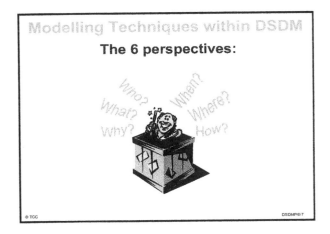

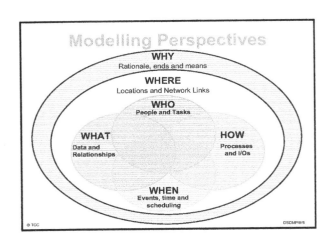

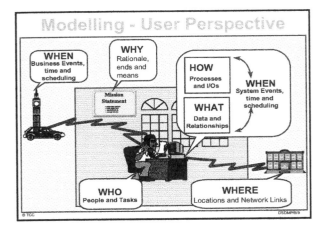

Notes

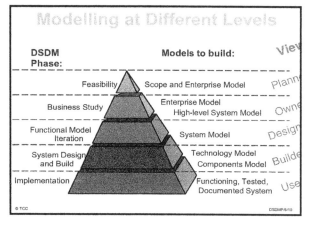

Modelling at Different Levels

DSDM Phase:	Models to build:	
Feasibility	Scope and Enterprise Model	View
Business Study	Enterprise Model / High-level System Model	Plann... / Own...
Functional Model Iteration	System Model	Design
System Design and Build	Technology Model / Components Model	Build...
Implementation	Functioning, Tested, Documented System	Use

© TCC   DSDMP/6/10

The DSDM Models Framework
Feasibility Study

DSDM Products	Objectives of Modelling What, How, Where, Who, When, Why	Examples of models	Examples of Interactions
Feasibility Report Feasibility Prototype Outline Plan	**Scope and Enterprise Model** • Key Data • Key Activities • Key Locations • Key People/Users • Key Events • Vision/Scope/ Objectives • Key Interfaces	**Core Models:** CSFs Context Diagram **Support Models:** Rich Picture Function Hierarchy Network Architecture Workflow Diagram Organisation Chart	Entity/Organisation Entity/Process Process/Location etc...

© TCC   DSDMP/6/11

Modelling Techniques

© TCC   DSDMP/6/12

Notes

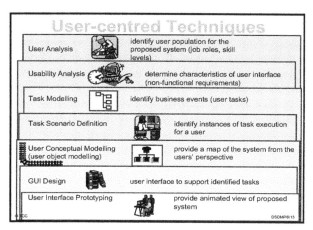

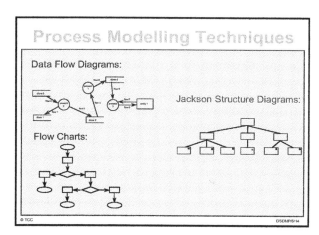

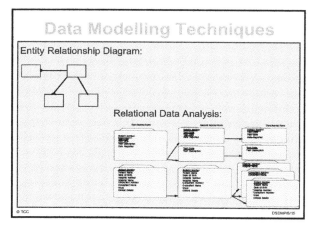

Notes

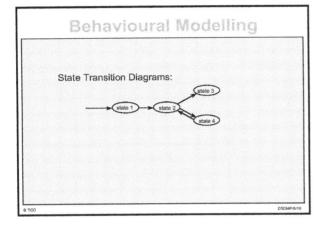

Behavioural Modelling

State Transition Diagrams:

© TCC — DSDMP/6/16

Techniques - Criteria for selection

- level of overhead

- easily understood by user and developer

- support process of serial refinement

- models produced must enhance communication

- must lie easily within the DSDM framework

© TCC — DSDMP/6/17

Modelling Technique
Criteria for DSDM

1. Software Engineering Discipline   8. Business Focus

2. Model Building Approach   9. User Focus

3. Model Refinement   10. Prototyping

4. Communication Aid   11. Non-functional Requirements

5. Re-use   12. Builds on Existing Knowledge

6. Traceability   13. Method Independence

7. DSDM Product Support   14. Requirements Management

© TCC — DSDMP/6/18

Session 7
Support Environments

1 DSDM Support Environments

A good support environment is essential to the success of the RAD approach. Tools for a DSDM project must encourage a dialogue between users and developers by allowing the developers to prototype and demonstrate their understanding of the users' requirements. Using only a 3GL programming language such as COBOL is not ideal when prototyping! However, for the DSDM approach to work successfully, the tool-set must lead to the development of a robust operational system.

Tool Support:

- is fundamental to RAD;

and consists of tools effectively used throughout the lifecycle, including (but not exclusively) the following:

- analysis and design tools;

- prototyping tools;

- configuration management tools;

- automated testing tools;

- automated documentation tools;

- code generators.

Ideally tool support should provide an integrated interface between all tools, a common data repository with communication between the tools.

The aim of this section is to identify some of the main characteristics of support environments for DSDM.

1.1 Ideal support environment

At the outset, it is worth stating that it is unlikely that any single tool will meet all the requirements. Therefore a range of tools may have to be used on any single development project. However, the range of requirements needs to be stated in the hope that one day such an environment will exist.

The diagram below shows an ideal integrated DSDM support environment. A number of "**Vertical**" tools support the various phases of a DSDM project from Feasibility Study through to Design and Build Iteration, including in some case the option of reverse engineering some legacy code. "**Horizontal**" tools provide support throughout the DSDM development process; such tools include configuration management and process control tools.

Such an environment provides integration at a number of levels:

- **Presentation**: provides a common "look and feel" across all tools;

- **Data**: differing tools share the same data repository;

- **Control**: one tool can notify and/or initiate actions in other tools;

- **Platform**: the tool set can be ported onto a number of differing platforms.

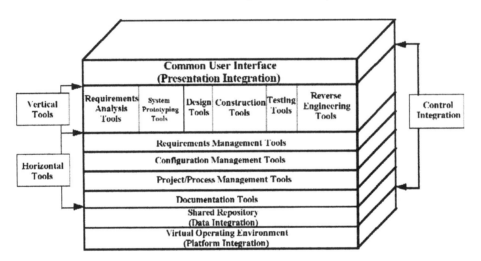

An ideal DSDM support environment

The inexperienced tool purchaser should be aware that many tool-set vendors have re-launched existing tool-sets as new RAD tools. In practice the functionality provided is very limited. In most cases, the tools support only rapid *program* development, which is only a small subset of rapid application development.

When selecting a DSDM support environment, the following steps are important:

- decide on your development process;

- select the techniques that support your process;

- decide on the required level of tool support.

Many organisations fail to achieve the most from their support tools by buying the tools before establishing the requirements.

Results from DSDM projects show that significant quality and productivity gains can be achieved from the use of inexpensive support tools. In particular in the areas of:

- code and schema generation;

- prototype generation;

- animation;

- automated document generation.

The ideal support environment does not yet exist but it is useful to consider a wish list for the ideal DSDM support environment. In this way organisations can select the tools which they must have, those which it would be nice to have and, of course, those which the organisation can afford.

The features which a tool can be assessed upon are discussed below:

1.1.1 Aids the process

Essentially any tool used in DSDM must not 'make life difficult'. Any information developed in one phase should be easily available to other phases.

1.1.2 Supports DSDM development techniques

The model building approach of DSDM and the associated models must be supported by the support environment.

1.1.3 Demonstrates usability

A good user interface will improve productivity from the tool and will encourage developers to use the tool enthusiastically. The quality of the tool will reveal itself in terms of:

- **Productivity**: what productivity gains are made by using the tool;

- **Learnability**: how easy it is for the user to become familiar with the tool;

- **User satisfaction**: how happy the user is in using the tool;

- **Memorability**: how easy it is for the user to remember how to use the tool;

- **Error rates**: the ability of the tool to decrease user-induced errors.

1.1.4   Openness

Since no one tool will meet all DSDM requirements it is essential that there is some way of passing information from one tool to another. In the PC environment OLE (Object Linking and Embedding) is the de facto standard to achieve this level of integration.

1.1.5   Supports user involvement

User involvement and participation are fundamental to the DSDM approach. The tools must not undermine this user involvement by intimidating the users.

1.1.6   Supports iteration

Any support environment for DSDM must support iteration and the possibility of return (backtracking) to previous versions of the developed system if the current incremental product is unsuitable for any reason. As an iteration is performed the new increment will have added new functionality to the system, or confirmed the user requirements for the system.

1.1.7   Baselining and version control

DSDM development is a very dynamic method with elements of the system potentially not only being developed at the same time but being at different stages of development at the same time. Different versions of the software may be installed at different sites if the organisation is multi-sited. New products and/or improvements are being generated at a much quicker rate than a traditional method would achieve, necessitating tight control over the products. Configuration Management is therefore essential (automated if possible) to avoid the chaos which could otherwise ensue.

1.1.8   Controlled repository

An open repository accessible by all tools within the support environment is desirable but within this there must be control. Different access rights (read-only, update) to the various products should be in place to ensure that one aspect of the development can not interfere with other aspects directly.

1.1.9   Supports reuse

It follows that, since DSDM seeks to produce systems in a short time frame, the reuse of previously developed products of other systems will help to shortcut the development time for new systems. The environment must allow the DSDM team to pick up these components and modify them for use in the developing system whilst the original version is retained in the 'reuse library'.

1.1.10   Navigation

Easy navigation or browsing around the developing system by developers working in different areas should be supported. Browsing through the reuse library to seek out useful components is also a desirable feature for the ideal support environment.

1.1.11   Documentation production

The whole of a DSDM project is directed toward rapid delivery. It follows that part of the delivery is the project documentation. It is all too easy to leave the documentation to last when the pressure is on. Automation is the key to improved productivity in this area.

1.1.12   Final system cut-over

One area where the most significant productivity gains can be made is in the production of the new system. The incremental delivery approach brings with it the problems of integrating these incremental products into the current system. The support environment should ease this process perhaps by allowing a prototype integrated system to be tested before release.

1.1.13   Multi-user

Whatever method is used for system development, it is true to say that the larger the system then the larger will be the development team. Support for multi-user development is therefore essential for rapid development.

1.1.14   Standardisation

The operating environment for the support tools should be consistent, for ease of use and promotion of an integrated tool set. Standardisation of the tools' interfaces will improve development team productivity.

1.1.15   Testing

Automated testing is a must to deliver working products with confidence. This testing is inter-threaded throughout the DSDM lifecycle and should be under user control. The kind of testing which should be supported is consistency checks between products as well as static and dynamic approaches.

1.2   Selecting a support environment

DSDM suggests a number of features of a support environment which should be investigated. This list is much the same as the approach that would be taken to package acquisition for any other application software. It includes such factors as supplier stability as well as the software features.

The main assessment criteria as suggested by DSDM are:

1.2.1   Supplier

The tool supplier should be well established and should have representatives within easy reach of the purchasing organisation. What do reference sites have to say of the supplier? The questions to ask are:

● Where has the tool been developed?

- Where is the distributor of the tool?

- What is the likelihood of delivery delays?

- Is an evaluation copy of the tool available?

- Does the supplier offer support/consultancy on the tool?

- Are there references from other installations?

1.2.2   Host environment

The environment of the tool must be considered. The questions to ask are:

- Does the tool run on different platforms?

- Can the tool be configured to work over a network of machines?

- Can the tool support multi-user operation, accessing the information concurrently?

- Does the host platform conform to the organisation's current IT Strategy?

- Is the hardware for the tool support environment the same as for the target environment? If not, will additional hardware have to be bought?

1.2.3   User support

The kind of support given by the tool must be investigated. The questions to ask:

- Does the user interface conform to local house style of interface?

- Is the tool simple to operate, and does it present information in a clear, precise manner?

- What are the response times like under high loading levels?

- What is the quality of the training documentation? Does the tool offer on-line help facilities?

- What length of learning curve is likely to be involved in using the tool? Is the supplier training considered to be sufficient?

- What is the quality of the user manuals? How much documentation is available?

- Are any reports available on the known bugs within the tool?

1.2.4 Price

What does the price of the tool include? Are training and maintenance costs included and therefore is the price within the project's budget for tool support?

1.2.5 Lifecycle Coverage

What facilities does the tool set offer to cover the phases in the DSDM development lifecycle? If the tool set does not offer total coverage then additional tools may have to be considered.

1.2.6 Techniques covered

What support does the tool offer for the preferred DSDM development techniques such as:

- Data Flow Diagrams;

- Entity Relationship Diagrams;

- State Transition Diagrams;

- Jackson Structure Charts;

- User Dialogues;

- Object-Orientation;

- Other techniques selected for the project.

1.2.7 Integrated techniques

Are the techniques integrated or does the information defined within one technique have to be re-entered within another? If a change is made to one model, are modifications to other models performed automatically?

1.2.8 Navigation

- Does the tool allow the user to navigate between the differing development models?

- Does the tool automatically navigate the user to the problem area of concern?

- Does the tool provide browsing of the repository for reusable components?

1.2.9 Consistency checking

- Does the tool ensure consistency of information within the tool database or provide facilities whereby it may be checked?

● What consistency checks are performed?

1.2.10 Open architecture

● Is the structure of the database made available to allow the developer to access the underlying database to enable additional checking and document preparation?

● Is the tool open? Can information be exported from the tool and can information be imported into the tool from other environments?

● Can the tool be interfaced to other support tools?

● Are there any restrictions on the size of the underlying database, concerning the number or type of data items that can be entered?

1.2.11 Documentation

Does the tool set offer facilities for printing documentation? The questions to ask are:

● Is documentation available for each technique, for example, entity descriptions, process descriptions?

● Can the information be generated in a form suitable for interfacing to a word processing system?

● Does the tool support the automatic production of documentation?

● Can differing document layouts and standards be defined?

● Does the tool support automatic code generation?

1.2.12 Change control

Does the tool offer facilities to cater for different versions of the defined system and provide an audit trail of changes made to the system?

1.2.13 Testing

What facilities are in place for testing DSDM products? The questions to ask are:

● Can the tool support the results of static testing?

● Can the tool support dynamic testing?

● Can the tool support regression testing?

1.3   Where are the productivity gains coming from?

Building the right system brings with it the productivity gains borne out of a reduced level of re-work and early detection of errors introduced through misunderstanding.

In the area of tool support environments major productivity gains are achievable through automation of:

- prototype generation;

- code and schema generation;

- automated document generation.

1.4   Implementation of the tools

The main expense in the use of support tools is probably incurred **after** the initial purchase. Some of the key activities that must be performed once the preferred RAD tool set has been selected include:

- **Training the Users**: all the users of the tool set will require some degree of training, whether it is formal training course or familiarisation time.

- **Rolling out the Tool Set**: a strategy is required for introducing the RAD tool set into the organisation, for example, on a project-by-project basis, or corporate wide.

- **Supporting the Tool Set**: an initial technical support team will be required to provide help desk support.

- **Developing Work-arounds**: once the preferred tool set has been used in a real project environment, several work-arounds will be required to accommodate differences with the organisation's development process, quality procedures and the interfaces between differing tool environments.

- **Monitoring the Use of the Tool Set**: once a tool set has been introduced into an organisation, it is important to monitor the use of the tool set; collect fault reports; determine whether the initial business benefits of introducing the Tool Set have actually been achieved.

2   Summary

For DSDM to achieve its full potential, for any particular project, there are a number of desirable pre-requisites. Earlier sessions have considered such factors as the importance of team structures, their roles and skills as well as other factors for a successful DSDM project. In this session, the major technique of prototyping has been discussed together with the support environment that will deliver many of the productivity gains that DSDM has the potential to deliver.

Notes

DSDM Support Environments

© TCC

DSDMP/7/1

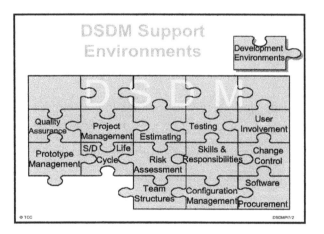

DSDM Support
Environments

Development
Environments

Quality
Assurance

Project
Management

Estimating

Testing

User
Involvement

Prototype
Management

S/D Life
Cycle

Risk
Assessment

Skills &
Responsibilities

Change
Control

Team
Structures

Configuration
Management

Software
Procurement

© TCC

DSDMP/7/2

DSDM Tool Support

Tool Support:

is fundamental to RAD

consists of:
  analysis & design tools
  prototyping tools
  configuration management tools
  automated testing tools
  automated documentation tools
  code generators
          etc ... etc ....

should ideally provide an integrated interface for all
tools, a common data repository, communication
between tools

© TCC

DSDMP/7/3

Notes

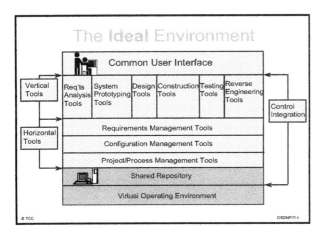

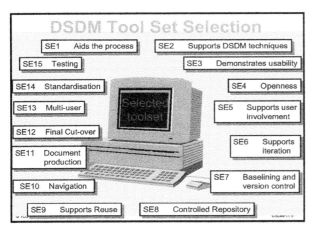

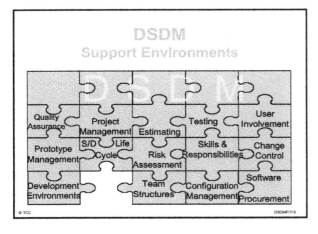

Session 8
Presentation and Negotiation Skills

Presentation Skills

1   Introduction

There will always be a place for written communication both within and between business organisations and to customers but, more and more, the importance of actually talking to people is being recognised. It will come as no surprise then, that throughout our careers we may find ourselves in situations requiring a presentation.

Having been tasked, our emotions are likely to be mixed – a combination of worry, apprehension and excitement. We must always remember that our audience will judge us, our organisation, and often our product by the quality of our presentation.

To give a good quality presentation there is a need for us to do a lot of planning and preparing which is a time-consuming business. However, if we approach the task systematically, we will produce a presentation that will interest, entertain and persuade our audience. This thorough preparation will also go a long way towards helping us to overcome our nerves. We will have far less to worry about if we know that the content is right. This session gives guidelines to help you produce an effective presentation.

2   The Presentation Pyramid

In order to structure your preparation, think of it as a pyramid, which has to be built from the base upwards. The layers of the pyramid are:

- plan;

- prepare;

- practice;

- deliver.

Follow these as your preparation sequence for the presentation.

3 Plan

3.1 Know your audience

You are sitting at your desk with a blank sheet of paper in front of you. You have probably written the title of your presentation at the top of the page. The ideas start to flow. You scribble frantically. But what about the audience? Put them first, if you want to be persuasive and memorable.

Who are they?

- customers?

- Board of Directors?

- graduate Trainees?

- members of the golf club?

- parent/teacher association?

How well do you know them?

- close colleagues?

- acquaintances?

- total strangers?

How many of them are there?

- a small intimate group?

- a sea of faces?

Why are they coming to listen to you?

- passive curiosity?

- urgent need to know?

- need to be convinced?

- they've been told to?

Level of knowledge

- what is their level of knowledge at the start of the presentation?

- where do you want it to be at the end?

3.2 Identify the central message

Look back to the title of your presentation – for example, "Introducing Flexible Working Time for all Administration Staff" – and think about how you might start off...

> *I'm here today to talk to you about introducing flexible working time for all administration staff.*

Clear enough, but not very inviting or memorable. You've taken a lot of trouble to find out about your audience. Use that knowledge to find an aspect of your proposal that will appeal to them. Identify the **purpose** and **benefit** to them. Then create your central message – a single, pithy sentence which tells your audience why you're giving the presentation and what's in it for them.

If you're talking to the staff...

> *Flexitime means that while your neighbours are sweating through the rush hour, you can be walking the dog.*

If you're talking to the Board...

> *With flexitime, you'll be open 11 hours a day with a crew of volunteers, and all it'll cost you is the electric light bill.*

4 Prepare

4.1 Gather information

Despite all the work you've done so far, finding out about your audience and creating a central message, you now need to gather the information which will form the content of your presentation.

Don't start to write your presentation yet. It will be wasted effort! Instead of a breakdown have a brainstorm.

Work out the topics to be covered, and what is essential or just nice to have. Talk to an audience member. What do they want?

If you are familiar with mind-maps or spider diagrams, try drawing one of these. This enables you to see the extent of the subject, links best ideas, sparks new ideas and highlights the key points relevant to your central message and therefore of benefit to your audience.

4.2 Select essential information

> *I could talk about it all night.*

Does that ring a bell? Knowing a lot can present more problems than knowing a little. The most dangerous subject is the one that fascinates you, and that you're the world expert on – leave your Anorak at home!!

Examine your own motives. Why are you including this point? Is it because your audience really wants or needs to know it, or is it just because you find it interesting?

Only choose points that really support your central message and make it more memorable.

Now put the information you've selected in two lists:

- vital to support your central message;

- useful to reinforce it if there's time.

Using this layout now will save you time later on if you need to alter or shorten your notes.

Whatever structure you choose, the most important thing is that you move logically from one section to the next and from one point to the next.

4.3   Organise venue

Book the venue and equipment for your presentation well in advance of your presentation, selecting a room of appropriate size for the expected number of attendees and the method of presentation.

4.4   Send invitations/pre-reading

People's time is in demand and to ensure that you have the right people at your presentation, send out invitations in good time. Background information should be issued where this will help clarify the issues and why individuals ought to be at the meeting.

4.5   Prepare your presentation

Sound preparation is the key to a good presentation of the information which you have selected to support your central message. A good structure forms the foundation.

4.5.1   Prepare the structure of the presentation

So you know what you want to say, but how are you going to structure it?

- **Situation**   Explain the background and the present position – yours and theirs.

- **Needs**   Show the audience that you have a good understanding of their needs; that you are aware of their problems.

- **Alternatives**   Outline the options that the audience has to improve the situation. Remember your solution isn't necessarily the only one.

- **Proposal**   Make your own case, linking it to the Central Message, to show how your audience will benefit.

4.5.2   Prepare the body of the presentation

This element of your presentation is where you build your central message for your audience. Unfortunately it is also the longest section and therefore the most likely period for your audience to flag unless you take steps to hold their attention.

It is not unusual during a presentation for an audience to lose concentration. The pattern will be the same no matter how long or short your overall presentation is. You are not going to get your message across if the audience isn't awake, attentive and active throughout. So you need to turn the attention troughs into peaks by making everything as clear and memorable as possible – the structure you've chosen, the talk time in minutes, the language you use, and the information you're presenting.

Look again at your structure. Break it down into sections to create more beginnings and endings since these are the periods when the audience's attention is at its best.

Now think about how to keep them with you when you move from section to section.

4.5.3   Prepare the introduction

"Good morning ladies and gentlemen..."

By now you've a pretty good idea of:

- what you want to cover;

- how you're going to cover it;

- how long it's going to take.

But how are you going to introduce yourself and the subject of your presentation?

It is useful to have a Route Map for your introduction:

- welcome;

- who I am;

- what "qualifies" me to speak;

- a synopsis of SNAP;

- how long it will take and the format;

- when I will be happy to take questions.

You should never include anything in your introduction that you will not include in the main body of your presentation.

4.5.4   Prepare the conclusion

So, Ladies and Gentlemen, just to sum up .....

By now, you should have the audience's full attention. This is the last chance to drive home your central message.

Don't add any new information at this stage: it'll only confuse. Just briefly restate your main points or proposal – using different words to avoid sounding repetitive. And try to finish on a high note.

Try and anticipate some of the questions you may get by thinking from the audience viewpoint, particularly if the group is made up of people from different job functions, e.g. a Marketing manager has a different viewpoint from that of a Finance Director. But don't attempt to answer all possible questions in your presentation. Get your messages across according to your objective and in the right time.

4.6   It's not just what you say, it's how you say it!

You've produced your plan; you've got a structure with a clear, punchy introduction, and a pithy conclusion. Is that enough to make sure you push the point home?

4.6.1   Signposting

A writer can show his reader that he's switching subjects, returning to an earlier theme, or concluding. He uses paragraphs. Presenters can't.

At every stage, tell your audience where they are, where they've been, and where they're going. Remember, your aim is to help them grasp your ideas easily, not battle with your logic.

Use signposts to:

- start a section (*OK. Let's start by...*)

- change sections (*Perhaps we could move on to the question of...*)

- reinforce the central message (*What does that mean to you?*)

- look ahead (*I'll come back to this point later*)

- look back (*As I mentioned earlier...*)

- link (*.. and that ties with...*)

- summarise (*So, what does it boil down to?*)

- conclude (*I think that covers everything*)

Use signposts too, to establish an understanding between you and your audience. Show them that you:

- understand their needs (*and this, of course, is why you want to...*)

- sympathise with their views (*You're absolutely right when you say...*)

- anticipate their questions (*You're probably wondering why we...*)

- appreciate their expertise (*I don't need to tell you that...*)

4.6.2   Use of language and painting pictures with words

Using concrete words, short sentences and word pictures usually works well and is particularly effective for emphasis of key points. This techniques can help to get your message across to your audience in a clear, punchy and concise way. But don't overdo it – use it as a variant for grabbing audience attention.

When you think of your favourite film, what springs first to mind? The actual words the actors used, or a visual impression of what went on? The visual memory is very powerful. Use it.

Paint word pictures – as wide a range as possible – with similes and visual analogies:

- *The control unit handles all interconnections in the system.*

- *Think of it as a telephone exchange serving a town.*

See how far you can extend it, without labouring the point (switchboards, party lines, engaged signals, phone numbers, bills):

- *If you want to send a message to another terminal, that's just like ringing a friend in the same town.*

Invite them to visualise the scene:

And there's Doris. You can hardly see her behind the mountain of paper in her in-tray. And she's trying to decide which of the four phones to answer first!

Put your points into a list of three, building up to a climax:

1. So, you're all aware there's a gap.

2. You know the gap has to be filled.

3. We have the way to fill it.

The rhythm of **3** works for individual words too:

- *It's going to be difficult, no question.*

- *But in the end it'll be efficient (1), modern (2) and,*

- *above all, profitable (3).*

Enhance the effect by using words with the same initial letter and sound:

- *It's going to be Painful, no question.*

- *But in the end it'll be Productive,*

- *Progressive and, above all, Profitable.*

If you want the audience to reject an alternative, build up a case for it, then knock it down with one or two sentences:

- *Sure it's cheap.*

- *Available from stock.*

- *Installation is no problem.*

- *User friendly too.*

    But...

- *It's totally incompatible with any other system.*

- *Take it, and you've lost all your flexibility.*

4.6.3   Prepare visual aids NOT liabilities

We've talked about making the structure clear and the language visual, but what about using visual aids themselves?

The range is wide. From real objects and samples, wall charts and pin boards, to slides, computer graphics and video tape. What resources do you have at your disposal to produce and show them?

Perhaps you're having your visual aids created and produced for you by experts, or perhaps you're putting them together yourself. There may be just an overhead projector in the presentation room, or a sophisticated computer and video system.

However simple or sophisticated your visual aids are, when should you use them? What should they look like? How should you show them?

Whatever visual aids you decide to use, you should ensure that you check each visual for size, colour, content and variety.

Will the audience be able to see and understand it from the back? Especially important to check if you're producing visuals from the printed page.

Experiment with different colour combinations and look at the results with a fresh eye. Which point do you want to highlight? Does it stand out better in red or black? What happens if you change the background colour?

Stick to one idea per visual and keep it uncluttered. Use it to throw light on an otherwise complex point.

You don't want all the visuals to look the same. Make them as varied as possible.

5 Practice

If you are well-prepared it will be self evident and you will take your audience logically through your presentation. A good way of preparing yourself is to...

- REHEARSE

- REHEARSE

- REHEARSE:

  - on your own – OUT LOUD;

  - in front of a mirror;

  - to a colleague(s);

  - to a family member(s).

Build rehearsal time into your preparation!

5.1 Voice and language

Think about your voice and the language you use:

- speed – not too fast or slow;

- strength of voice – speaking too loudly is not a problem but mumbling, garbling and whispering is;

- pitch – this can give emphasis to key points;

- pace – change the pace;

- pause – to allow assimilation of ideas;

- keep it simple – avoid jargon;

- use (the right sort of) humour;

- smile;

- explain the whole before the parts.

Remember, variety will hold your audience's attention.

Check the timing.

5.2 Checking body language

Again, a colleague might be able to help you here.

Any mannerisms that you have (head scratching, pacing up and down, fiddling about in your pocket, waving your hands around) are fine unless the audience finds them more interesting than what you're saying.

Throat clearing, ahs and hms between sentences, verbal tics (you know? OK? yeah? sort of, right?) can distract or irritate if they're too frequent.

6 Deliver

6.1 Making the final checks – pre-delivery

- Have you got your notes in order?

- Are they legible?

- Have you checked your timing?

- Are you sure you're not going to speak for too long?

- Are you using visuals? If so, are they in order?

- What about the equipment? Have you tried it out? Is it in the right position? Can you use it without fumbling?

- Have you checked the room?

- Where will you be standing or sitting?

- Will they be able to hear you and see you from the back? Have you got a microphone?

- Is the lighting OK?

- Is everything else you might need – paper, pens, pointers – to hand?

- Have you got enough copies of any hand-outs you're giving them at the end?

6.2 Using your visuals

When it comes to showing the visuals within your presentation there are a number of tips which help to make their use effective:

- Be sensitive. Either you prepared your own visual, or you know it extremely well, but your audience hasn't seen it before.

- Position yourself so that everyone can see. You don't want the Managing Director craning his neck or squinting. If you're right handed, stand with the visual on your right.

- Signpost each visual briefly before you show it to them.

- Stay quiet while they absorb it before you start talking. A simple graph with two axes, one curve and a title takes at least 7 seconds to absorb and understand; and that's assuming the audience are used to such visuals.

- Then make your point and explain. Keep your eyes on the audience and talk to them, not the visual – even if their eyes are not on you.

- Switch off the machine or take the visual away when you've finished with it.

Remember, you need about two minutes per visual: to put it up, to give the audience time to absorb it, then to explain it and draw conclusions from it. So, make sure you haven't got too many. Strike a balance between visual aids and apt analogies.

6.3 Eye contact

Make an effort not to look at the ceiling or floor. The audience will sense your confidence has gone.

Remember to look at the audience and not your visual aid.

Look around and establish eye contact, even with the people who are sitting at the sides of the room. If you focus on the person in front of you, you'll make him feel guilty and the others will switch off.

6.4 Handling questions

Assessing how your message is being received can be done in two major ways. Looking at the physical reaction of the group i.e. their body language, and seeing what questions are asked.

If you are interrupted with a question you don't want to answer at that time, explain why and when you will answer it. Note the question down and remember to answer it at the right time. Refer specifically to the question to show them that this is their answer.

Questions are a positive sign of interest and allow us to check the group's understanding. When handling questions from the floor, follow this procedure:

- listen carefully to the question and note it down if necessary;

- thank the questioner;

- check that you understand it – if necessary ask for more information or re-phrase or translate it;

- give your answer – be brief, think first of your answer so that you are concise;

- check you have answered fully;

- thank them again

A question session at the end shows you have stimulated the group to think seriously about your presentation.

7 Summary of Presentation Skills

Remember:

- Plan;

● Prepare;

● Practice;

● Deliver.

but especially remember:

FAILURE TO PREPARE IS PREPARATION TO FAIL

8 Negotiation

8.1 Negotiation is about people

Negotiation is a process in which ego and emotions can easily become involved but we should be conscious of the impact of such emotion on our negotiating ability. **Always keep in mind the objective issues that are involved.** When we allow emotions to get carried away with us the entire process is undermined or real issues are sacrificed in order to satisfy emotional needs. Carried too far, the desire to be the winner in a negotiation will necessarily mean that the other party is a loser.

Negotiation is about developing and managing relationships during the negotiation. It is possible to be hard-nosed and tough, and still establish a good relationship with high levels of credibility. The key is to separate the conflict elements, which are business-driven, from positive personal elements, which relate to you and the other party as people.

Don't forget that the negotiating process can, for many people, be one of the most stressful aspects of a relationship. What occurs during the negotiating process may well have a major impact on the long-term relationship that you are establishing.

8.2 The four stages of negotiation

There are four stages to any negotiation each of them critical to a successful (for both parties) outcome of the negotiation process. These are:

● Prepare;

● Discuss;

● Propose;

● Bargain.

We will now look at each of these stages in more detail.

8.3 Prepare

8.3.1 Negotiation planning is never wasted.

Occasionally we get a nice surprise. We plan extensively for a negotiation only to find that the other party agrees with all or most of our position. Wonderful! Close the deal and move on to the next. You didn't waste your time planning. If there had been major opposition, you would have been ready.

A few common sense rules will help prepare for the negotiation by reducing conflict, turning it into cooperation to allow solutions that really work for **all** the participants to be reached.

8.3.2 Separate the people from the problem.

If we view the problem as that which needs to be resolved rather than viewing someone holding a contrary viewpoint as a person to be defeated, the odds of a successful negotiation increase. One simple idea, executed in preparing the venue for the negotiation, is to change the shape of the table; rather than sitting opposite your 'opponents', arrange the seating so that all the parties are sitting together facing a flip chart or whiteboard, where the problem is presented. The covert message is that all the participants are facing the problem together – instead of it being 'us' against 'them', it is a case of 'all of us' against 'it'.

8.3.3 Distinguish between interests and positions

Consider the story of two sisters fighting over the only orange in the fruit bowl. Each sister must have the entire orange for herself – apparently any less is impossible. A wise negotiator asks each of the girls (in private) why she wants the orange. One explains she wants to drink the juice; the other wants to use the rind to cook a pudding. What each sister wants is her **position**, why she wants it is her **interest**. In this case, the simple solution is to give the cook the rind after the juice has been squeezed for the thirsty sister – thus meeting the interests of both is possible although their initial position was one of conflict.

8.3.4 Planning

When preparing for a negotiation don't just ask "What do they want?" It is also important to ask, "Why do they want it?" It is equally important, and often more difficult to ask the same questions of yourself. Many successful negotiators find they will be more successful if they focus on understanding their interests as they enter discussions. If they start out with an open mind, the ideas of others may actually improve their final result.

Prepare your objectives, what you wish to achieve and alternative ways of achieving them. Decide which objectives are fixed and which have some flexibility within which you can negotiate.

Plan the negotiation sequence raising less contentious issues first and try to anticipate the likely response of the other party to your issues.

Do not prepare a complete package. Negotiators who arrive with a complete package can create real problems. Modifications to their ideas might be taken personally, they may be stubborn, and reaching a satisfactory resolution is made more difficult.

8.4 Discuss

Once the negotiation process has entered the discussion phase both parties are trying to gather information about the other's position whilst sitting at the negotiating table. By understanding the other party's position and interests you are equipping yourself with what needs to be achieved to satisfy the other party's needs, not that all of them may be satisfied of course! Questioning can be open or closed, but should certainly seek to probe and elicit relevant information.

During this and subsequent phases people are signalling and it is very important to watch for these signals as the negotiation proceeds. Sometimes signals are overt and quite clear, but often they are subtle and easy to miss. But these signals can be of three types:

- Signals that people intend to send and that are true. Instead of saying things outright the information is given while preserving some degree of deniability – "I didn't actually say that";

- Second, there are signals that people intend to send that are false. These signals are calculated to mislead you and direct you away from the other party's true goals;

- Third, the unintentional signal that slips out, can provide critical information on what they want or will accept. These unintended signals can be very valuable, provided that you can distinguish them from the misleading ones!!

Sometimes a negotiator can act or appear to be irrational, use anger and intimidation, use jargon, and so forth to throw the other negotiating party and compromise their ability to negotiate effectively. Occasionally you will encounter a situation where an individual is truly upset or angry. In such a case it is important to deal with the emotional aspects before trying to continue with the process.

Active listening is a crucial tool in the negotiation process. If you do not actively listen, how can you get a clearer picture of the other party's ideas? And when the listener's response shows just how good a job he or she has done listening, it can shock the other party

"Good grief, they actually paid attention to me!"

Active listening forces a disciplined approach to focus on other opinions, giving the listener the chance to reflect on the process and strategy. The discipline of active listening requires that you focus on what another person is saying; don't spend your time shaping a stinging response that will put them in their place. Stepping aside and taking a dispassionate view of the goings-on can make one a far more effective negotiator.

Implied in active listening is that the listener has to be silent. You can't talk and listen at the same time and therefore understand the other party's opinion. In turn you won't be able to make an intelligent response to an opinion you do not understand.

Silence can be as effective a tool as speech. If one party is highly opinionated or emotional, if their approach is threatening or extremely demanding, keeping quiet after they finish speaking can be quite unsettling to them. Most people are troubled by silence in the midst of heated discussion. Sometimes silence is viewed as disapproval — but since no specific disapproval has been voiced, it cannot be treated as an attack. It has happened on many occasions that, when met with silence, people have modified their previous statements to make them more palatable!!

It takes at least two to argue! To help individuals keep a cool head and pay attention to the process and the strategy, as well as the substance of the negotiation only one person should be allowed to become angry at any one time, although it is preferable that no one gets to this emotional state. Yelling at each other is not negotiation; it is confrontation. In those situations there may possibly be a 'winner'; but it is even more likely there will be a 'loser'. If it's not your 'turn' to be angry, the exercise of restraint can be turned into a positive opportunity to observe what is going on with a clear eye.

8.5 Propose

Each party may make proposal and counter-proposal during the negotiation process with each of these becoming the boundaries between which compromise and negotiation can be enacted.

Sometimes a deadlock can occur – in fact negotiation may be considered to be a process of managing a series of short-term deadlocks. We declare a negotiation "deadlocked," and that may appear to be an end to it. It appears that there is no reasonable expectation for enough further movement on either side to bridge the remaining gap between the parties. If, however, you determine that you still wish to see the negotiation continue, there are a number of steps that you can take to accomplish this:

- move the discussion away from the deadlock zone by changing issues;

- try to find agreements in principle;

- adjourn but do not end the negotiating session;

- bring in other parties;

- develop new information;

- move to a more informal setting.

Any means to take any heat, disappointment, exhaustion, frustration and so on out of the process can bring renewed determination and vigour to the negotiation and allow a bargain to be achieved.

8.6   Bargain

Bargaining can only be successful if all participants perceive the process as fair. Particpants are more likely to take it seriously and 'buy into' its result if this is the case. Moreover, the focus on fairness can have an important impact on the substantive result.

The notion before or even after a negotiation that "we really stuffed them" embodies a recognised sense of calculated unfairness that will leave the "stuffed" party aggrieved in the very least. To be considered successful, an agreement must be durable and parties who walk away from the table grumbling may subsequently regret their commitment and only honor it grudgingly. If they end up looking for excuses to get out from under an unwanted result, the gains achieved by the other side may prove to be short-term indeed.

In bargaining, the phrase of the format "If we provide... then perhaps you could do... for us" is a useful tool to bring parties closer to agreement. Try to concede things that are 'cheap' for you to give but 'worth a lot' to the other party.

It is very common in the negotiating process for the agreement to come together at the last minute. To the outside observer it may appear as though nothing is happening, and then all at once, at the 11th hour, an agreement materialises. This occurs in part because of the need for an early feeling-out process during which time no agreements are reached and in part because each side is waiting for the other side to make concessions first. Neither side sees a reason to concede until time pressures force them to do so at the last minute.

Another pattern that is quite common is for the parties to reach agreement on some of the easier issues early on in the process while the remaining difficult issues are resolved at the last minute.

Be aware of these patterns, be patient, and don't assume that because you are reaching the end of the time available that there will be a deadlock.

The ideal outcome from a negotiation meeting is the scenario where both parties feel that they have won: the "WIN-WIN" outcome. Each party may not have won everything that they had wished for but through a series of discussion, proposal and bargaining phases it is possible to explore the flexibilities in each party's interests and arrive at an agreement that brings significant benefits to both parties.

Notes

Presentation and Negotiation Skills

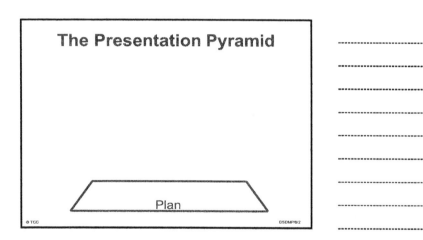

The Presentation Pyramid

The Presentation Pyramid

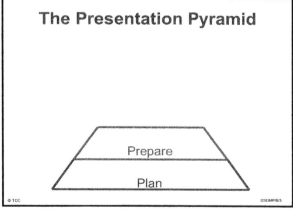

Notes

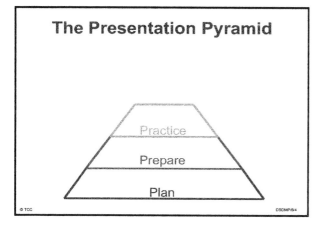

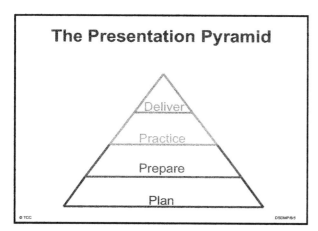

Plan

- **Know your Audience**

  Where do they start?
  Where should they be at end?

- **Identify Central Message**

  Purpose + Benefit

Notes

Prepare

- Gather information

- Select essential information

- Organise venue

- Send Invitations/pre-reading

© TCC   DSDMP/9/7

Prepare
Order of Preparation

- Body

- Introduction

- Conclusion

© TCC   DSDMP/9/8

Prepare
Structure of Presentation

- S ituation

- N eed

- A lternatives

- P roposal

© TCC   DSDMP/9/9

Notes

**Prepare
Structure of Presentation**

- **P** resent position

- **P** roblems we face

- **P** ossibilities

- **P** roposal

© TCC · · · · · · · · · · · · DSDMP/8/10

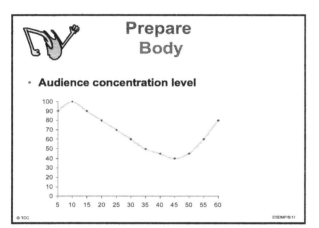

**Prepare
Body**

- **Audience concentration level**

© TCC · · · · · · · · · · · · DSDMP/8/11

**Prepare
Body**

- **Maintaining audience concentration level**

How?

© TCC · · · · · · · · · · · · DSDMP/8/12

Notes

Prepare
Introduction

- Who are you?
- What qualification?
- SNAP
- Length and format
- When questions taken

© TCC   DSDMP/9/13

Prepare
Conclusion

- Finish on time
- Summarise (nothing new)
- What action now required
- Questions

© TCC   DSDMP/9/14

Prepare
Visual Aids

- Flipchart
- OHP and transparencies
- Desktop projector
- LCD panel
- 35mm slides
- Other?

© TCC   DSDMP/9/15

Notes

---

poor reveal

What makes a bad Visual Aid?

too small - this is 12 point but this is 20 point

too many fonts   wwrroonnggffoonntt

wrong emphasis

wrong colours

inakurat speling

too much information   use of graphics is a better idea than loads
of text which is difficult to read in block especially
from the back of a large room. Text should really be kept
to a few key words and not a nobel-prize-winning essay.
Graphics should be *relevant* to be memorable. (Phew!)

© TCC   DSDMP/8/16

Practice (1)

• **Rehearse alone**

• **Dry-run with audience**

• **Keywords (cards?)**

• **Use of voice/emphasis**

© TCC   DSDMP/8/17

What people remember about you

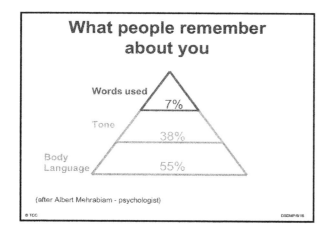

Words used   7%

Tone   38%

Body Language   55%

(after Albert Mehrabiam - psychologist)

© TCC   DSDMP/8/18

Notes

Practice (2)

- Body language

- Appearance

- Anticipate questions

- Timing

© TCC   DSDMP/8/19

Final checks

✓ Notes in order?
✓ Timing OK?
✓ Visual aids in order
✓ Equipment checked?
✓ Room checked?
✓ Sufficient hand-outs?
✓ Is the reason for the presentation still valid?

© TCC   DSDMP/8/20

Deliver
Order of Presentation

- Introduction

- Body

- Conclusion

© TCC   DSDMP/8/21

Notes

Question Handling

- Listen
- Thank
- Check understanding

- Give answer
- Check satisfaction
- Thank again

If you don't know, say so!

© TCC

DSDMP/8/22

Presentation Skills Summary

Deliver

Practice

Prepare

Plan

Remember: Failure to prepare is preparation to fail!

© TCC

DSDMP/8/23

The Presentation Pyramid

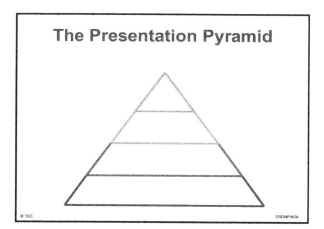

© TCC

DSDMP/8/24

Notes

Negotiation

- Prepare

- Discuss

- Propose

- Bargain

© TCC   DSDMP/8/25

Negotiating Skills

- Look at the person

- Inquire with questions

- Stay on Target

- Test Understanding

- Evaluate the negotiation process

- Neutralise feelings

© TCC   DSDMP/8/26

Negotiating Skills
Questions

Directive

Probing (who, what, why, where, when, how)

?

Open/Closed   Leading

© TCC   DSDMP/8/27

Notes

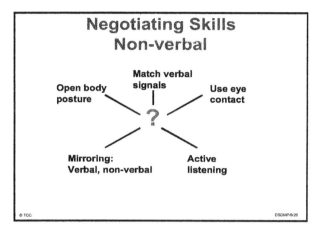

Session 9
Making DSDM Successful

1 Introduction

There are three major issues which must be considered to ensure that the introduction of DSDM is successful:

- the characteristics of the organisation;

- how should DSDM be introduced;

- risks and benefits.

2 Characteristics of the Organisation

Introducing a new system development method into an organisation is like introducing anything new. Change is something which people are reluctant to accept for a variety of reasons, not least of which is the fear of not being able to cope with it.

The characteristics of an organisation can be broken down into a number of relevant considerations:

- its culture;

- the level of bureaucracy;

- the physical environment;

- the system development environment;

- the skill levels.

2.1 The culture

The culture of the organisation as a whole as well as that of the IT department may embody either flexible or rigid working practices. DSDM is a flexible method, which could be quite alien within an environment where job descriptions are enacted in a restrictive fashion. If Management is very much in control, perhaps even dictatorial, DSDM will be somewhat of a culture shock to them. Here is an approach where they are expected to relinquish control of some IT projects to the team, which is going to develop the system. For their part, the development team will be inhibited and fearful of overstepping the mark, which will stifle innovation and slow the RAD process. It will also be difficult for user managers to accept that their staff will be taken out of their departmental job role 'to help out the IT department'.

The key to facing up to the challenge in this type of culture is for Senior Management (including IT and user managers) to show its commitment to the DSDM method and the benefits which it will bring. To obtain this commitment may require senior management to attend some form of DSDM overview course, which is designed to fire them with enthusiasm. They will then go back to affirm their commitment to the individuals who will form the team. Once team members have been given approval and guaranteed the support of user managers in allowing staff to leave their departmental job to actively develop a new system for the department, the groundwork is in place.

The success of the DSDM project (once a suitable project has been identified) will however require this verbal assertion of support to be enacted – words into action. The project manager must ensure that this happens.

2.2 The level of bureaucracy

DSDM is about delivering quality applications rapidly and anything, which compromises either of these, is a risk to successful implementation of the DSDM method. It follows then that if the organisation is burdened by bureaucracy the project manager is going to find it very difficult to drive the project along. The team should be self-directed and empowered with no bureaucratic drag upon the process.

2.3 The physical environment

The major activities, which are fundamental to the operation of DSDM, are prototyping and JAD sessions. It follows then that for prototyping sessions the user-developer team must be physically able to gather around a workstation to prototype the application. Likewise for JAD sessions there needs to be a room large enough to accommodate up to twelve participants, comfortably. The room should be equipped with at least one of, an OHP, flipchart and whiteboard. These will be used during the JAD as a means of recording issues as a memory aid for the facilitator. The major recording activities of course are carried out by the scribe(s)

2.4 The system development environment

The System Development Environment has to be in place for DSDM to be possible. Tool support is critical to a successful implementation of DSDM and therefore the environment has to be in place before the project is started.

2.5 The skill levels

As stated earlier there is no provision in DSDM for the acquisition of the necessary skills to implement it. Training can be purchased and experience bought in for early projects but much of the expertise in the development and support tools should be already in place.

3 How Should DSDM be Introduced?

The first project, which will take the DSDM approach, should be carefully selected to 'pilot the method'. After all, this will be the proving ground if the method is to be adopted for future use within the organisation. The right project will be the one, which is identified as having the best chance of success. It must be a "real" project in the sense of it being important (vital!).

So what factors other than DSDM's applicability are important in selecting the right project? If management commitment is not forthcoming then the project and DSDM are fated. By selecting a Senior Manager who is desperate for a new system and believes in the benefits, which IT can bring the first hurdle, has been crossed. The next step is to convince the manager that DSDM will deliver benefits to his/her department quickly and that the quality will be high. Having identified the right project with the right manager the project can be initiated.

The next step is to identify the best mix of **enthusiastic** developers and users, matching their skills and personalities in relation to the necessary DSDM roles. This will secure their personal commitment, which can then be backed up by the commitment of their manager to make them available as the project requires.

Bringing the DSDM Project Team together for training in DSDM initiates the team building exercise. It is important to assess the skill levels of the developers to ensure that they can use the techniques and tools that will be used on the project and that configuration management procedures are in place. If a tool or technique is to be used for the first time on the project it may be advisable to bring external expertise in as required.

The developer members can give user awareness training in the techniques and tools just before they are to be used. This will continue the team building process.

The appropriate DSDM products can be identified and the sizing of timeboxes established so that dates of reviews, Facilitated Workshops, demonstrations, etc. can be scheduled into everybody's diaries early. The agreed plan has then to be adhered to without losing sight of the fact that the delivery date is fixed.

The last point to make is that the project manager should keep in mind and therefore guard against the risks that can affect a DSDM project.

3.1 Action Plan for implementing DSDM

The Action Plan for introducing DSDM can be found in the DSDM Version 3 Manual, which is available from the DSDM Consortium. This provides a useful checklist for any organisation considering using DSDM.

4 Risks and Benefits

4.1 Risks of using DSDM

The risks of using DSDM are discussed fully in an earlier session. but are repeated here as a reminder:

- lack of necessary level of <u>consistent</u> user involvement;

- time spent in decision-making endangers the project;

- team members become focused on activities;

- deliverables are not "fit for purpose";

- iteration and incremental activities not controlled;

- backtracking is difficult or impossible;

- high-level requirements are not baselined;

- testing is not integrated throughout life-cycle;

- not all stakeholders have collaborative, co-operative approach.

4.2 Benefits of DSDM

The use of an iterative approach to system development within a prototyping environment and involving users in a very active way brings many benefits:

- the users are more likely to claim ownership for the system;

- the risk of building the wrong system is greatly reduced;

- the final system is more likely to meet the users' real business requirements;

- the users will be better trained;

- the system implementation is more likely to go smoothly.

5 Conclusion

DSDM is an evolving RAD method which can deliver significant business benefits in a shorter time than a traditional method. It relies upon animated modelling and strong teamwork between user team members and developer team members. DSDM Consortium members are reporting significant savings in development effort and therefore cost savings. As experience in using the method is gained the refinement of the method together with refined combinations of toolset and techniques will result in even greater benefits being possible.

Notes

MAKING DSDM SUCCESSFUL

© TCC   DSDMP/9/ 1

Cultural Change

Where are we now?

- How are projects currently staffed? Grade-conscious?
- Project Manager "clout"?
- Consensus or regulation?
- Flexible developers?
- Staff mobility?
- Can workshops be accommodated?
- Operations staff responsive?
- Development environment right for prototyping?

© TCC   DSDMP/9/ 2

Introducing DSDM
- A Plan of Action

1.   **Identify a DSDM Champion.**

© TCC   DSDMP/9/ 3

Notes

Introducing DSDM
- A Plan of Action

2. Communicate the philosophy and concepts of DSDM to all concerned.

© TCC   DSDMP/9/4

Introducing DSDM
- A Plan of Action

3. Examine the current development practices and procedures and compare with DSDM approach.

© TCC   DSDMP/9/5

Introducing DSDM
- A Plan of Action

4. Identify areas that will need to be changed.

© TCC   DSDMP/9/6

Notes

Introducing DSDM
- A Plan of Action

5. Gain support and commitment for the plan.

© TCC   DSDMP/9/7

Introducing DSDM
- A Plan of Action

6. Identify first project.

© TCC   DSDMP/9/8

Introducing DSDM
- A Plan of Action

7. Train the project team.

© TCC   DSDMP/9/9

Notes

Introducing DSDM
- A Plan of Action

8. Set up the development environment.

© TCC   DSDMP/9/10

Introducing DSDM
- A Plan of Action

9. Launch the project.

© TCC   DSDMP/9/11

Introducing DSDM
- A Plan of Action

10. Run first project.

© TCC   DSDMP/9/12

Notes

Notes

---

14. **Prepare for the next DSDM projects.**

© TCC · DSDMP/9/16

---

15. **Measure the business benefits.**

© TCC · DSDMP/9/17

- lack of necessary level of consistent user involvement
  - time spent in decision-making endangers the project schedule
- focus on activities rather than products
  - deliverables not fit for purpose
- iteration is not well-controlled
  - backtracking difficult or impossible
- high-level requirements not baselined
  - testing not integrated throughout the life cycle
- co-operative collaboration is not everyone's agenda

© TCC · DSDMP/9/18

Notes

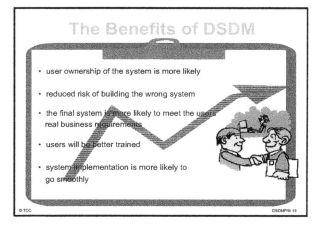

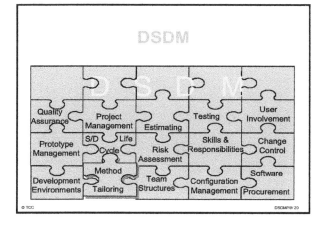

Appendix A
Software Procurement (Outsourcing)

1 Introduction

If the decison is made to outsource the development of bespoke software the customer (purchasing organisation) often prefers a fixed price for the development in order to allocate their budget. For their part, the supplier (vendor organisation) will usually accept this provided that the Requirements Specification is detailed enough to form the basis for contractual agreement. What's in the specification is included in the fixed price, what's not included is subject to further negotiation (and therefore cost).

Of course DSDM is not like this. The specification is not fixed and depends upon a flexible approach with evolutionary requirements. From the supplier point of view, they can operate flexibly but to sign a fixed price contract could see them being a 'hostage to fortune'. For this reason DSDM recommends that development contracts should be carried out on a **time and materials basis.**

The problems of outsourcing a development within a DSDM framework are therefore:

- fixed price contractual agreements embody a performance delivery ethos which makes the development process rigid;

- suppliers may feel uncomfortable with the DSDM approach, perhaps through unfamiliarity, or the lack of protection, from unreasonable user expectation that would be provided by a detailed specification;

- whilst suppliers are more comfortable with a detailed specification for a fixed price Invitation to Tender (ITT), the time and cost to produce such a specification is significant, perhaps even as long as the time which the DSDM project itself would have taken to complete!

2 Fixed Price Contracts

Whilst DSDM recommends 'time and materials' and the foregoing discussion may suggest that fixed price developments are not possible within DSDM, there is a way forward for fixed price contracts and DSDM.

In order to consider a fixed price contract it is essential for there to be a good project manager from the customer side together with a good project manager from the supplier side. Both must be empowered to make desisions on behalf of their respective organisations and between them they must be able to build a sound trusting relationship.

As noted previously, new requirements emerge during prototyping in DSDM and the two project managers must be able to agree whether these requirements are inside or outside the initial scope of the contract. If they are outside, then the effort required to incorporate them is estimated and the cost is calculated based on the daily rate agreed for such eventualities when the contract was first set up.

As a guide to whether a requirement can be considered to be in the initial scope of the project it may be helpful to consider the following:

A requirement can be considered to be outside the scope if:

- a new high level process has to be added to the DFD set;

- a new entity has to be added to the Entity Relationship Diagram (ERD);

- it is a non-functional requirement not identified in Business Study.

The use of external suppliers does not change the basic premise that DSDM will allow the functionality to be de-scoped leaving out non-essential requirements which arise from prototyping sessions. The development must be completed within the tight timescales set for it and therefore even though the new requirements may be within the original scope, it does not mean that they will all be completed within the fixed price. It is important that the project managers appreciate each other's point of view and that a co-operative approach is adopted.

3 Alternative Contracts (The Hybrid Approach)

If the customer is not happy with an open-ended time and materials basis and the supplier is not happy with the open commitment which he perceives DSDM to promote, then it is possible to reach a compromise. If compromise can not be achieved then perhaps the supplier is not the right organisation to co-operate with on a DSDM project, or maybe the customer wants to 'have his cake and eat it'.

At this stage the type of relationship which is, or is not, possible will become clear and either party may choose to withdraw.

If both parties seek a compromise there are a number of possible hybrid contracts which can keep both customer and supplier happy and remain compliant with the objectives of DSDM. These are discussed below.

3.1 Fixed price per timebox

Initially an estimate is agreed by supplier and customer for the whole project. As each timebox is about to commence a fixed price is agreed, its accuracy being measured against the actual cost. The fixed price for subsequent timeboxes can then be adjusted in line with this comparison and agreed by both parties on an on-going review basis. There are two benefits to this. Firstly the supplier is not pinned down on price for the whole project and secondly the customer can call a halt at any stage to avoid serious overspend whilst still having the incrementally delivered parts for which payment has beeen made.

3.2 Fix the number of iterations and their length

At the start of the project the number of, and length of, the iterations is fixed allowing a fixed price contract to be agreed.

3.3 The incentive fee contract

The most likely price is agreed for the DSDM development. If there is underspend on the project, then this will be shared between the supplier and the customer in some previously agreed proportions. This gives the supplier the incentive to complete the work in a timely manner with a reward for completing the work early. Conversely if there is overspend the customer pays the supplier at a reduced daily rate agreed at the outset. This acts as a check on rampant growth of the requirements list.

3.4 Time and materials followed by fixed price

Initially in a DSDM it can be difficult for both parties to estimate the size of the job. In the early stages it may be fairer for both parties to carry out the initial work on a time and materials basis. Once a defined point in the functional model (scope better understood) has been reached, a fixed price can be quickly agreed by both parties for the remainder of the work.

3.5 First increment on time and materials, then fixed

This is very similar in principle to the previous approach but is based on producing the first incremental product on a time and materials arrangement. Thereafter the customer and supplier have a better understanding of the scope of the project and fixed price agreements can be made for delivery of subsequent increments.

4 The Procurement Process

The procurement process is not at all unlike that followed for a traditional method. After the completion of the DSDM Business Study the customer should go out to several suppliers for their recommended solution and costings. This competitive bid will usually be in response to an Invitation to Tender (ITT) document issued in line with the DSDM guidelines. The supplier responds with a vendor proposal which, again, is in line with DSDM guidelines.

When all bids have been received, the customer evaluates the proposals and selects the most appropriate solution. It is then up to the customer and supplier to manage their relationship within the DSDM framework.

Appendix B
Recommended Reading

DSDM Consortium

Dynamic Systems Development Method V3 Manual, 1995, available from:

The DSDM Consortium
Invicta Business Centre
Monument Way
Orbital Park
Ashford
Kent
TN24 0HB
Tel: +44 (0)1233 501300
Fax: +44 (0)1233 501311

RAD

Kerr, J. and Hunter, R.

"Inside RAD: How to build fully functional computer systems in 90 days or less, McGraw-Hill, 1994

Martin, J.

Rapid Application Development, Maxwell Macmillan International Editions, 1991, ISBN 0-020376775-8

Stapleton, J.

DSDM: The Method in Practice, Addison Wesley Longman, 1997, ISBN 0-201-17889-3

Methods, Techniques and People

Ashworth, C. and Slater, L.

An Introduction to SSADM Version 4, McGraw-Hill, 1992, ISBN 0-07-707725-3

Boehm, B.W.

Software Engineering Economics, Prentice-Hall, 1981, ISBN 0-13-822122-7

Belbin, R.M.

Management Teams: Why they Succeed or Fail, Butterworth-Heinemann, 1981

Belbin, R.M.

Team Roles at Work, Butterworth-Heinemann, 1993, ISBN 0-7506-0925-7

Date, C.

An Introduction To Database Systems, Addison-Wesley, 1986, ISBN 0-201-19215-2

Eason, K.   Information Technology and Organisational Change, Taylor & Francis, 1989 ISBN 0-85066-388-1

Gilb, T.   Principles of Software Engineering Management, Addison-Wesley, 1988, ISBN 0-201-19246-2

Goodland, M. and Slater, C.   SSADM Version 4 – A Practical Approach, McGraw-Hill, 1995, ISBN 0-07-709073-X

Hix, D. and Hartson, H.R.   Developing User Interfaces: Ensuring Usability through Product and Process, Wiley, 1993, ISBN 0-471-53846-9

Jacobson, I., Christerson, M.,   Object Oriented Software Engineering, Addison
Jonsson, P. and Overgaard, G.   Wesley, 1992, ISBN 0-201-54435-0

Jacobson, I., Ericsson, M. and   The Object Advantage – Business Process Re-engineering
Jacobson, A   with Object Technology, Addison-Wesley, 1995, ISBN 0-201-42289-1

Paulk, M.C., et al   Capability Maturity Model for Software Version 1.1, Software Engineering Institute, Technical report CMU/SEI-93-TR24, 1993 (Note: CMU is Carnegie Mellon University, Pittsburgh)

Rumbaugh, J., Blaha, M.,   Object-Oriented Modelling and Design,
Premerlani, W., Eddy, F.   Prentice-Hall, 1991, ISBN 0-13-630054-5
and Lorensen, W

Shlaer, S. and Mellor, S.J.   Object-Oriented Systems Analysis, Yourdon Press, 1988, ISBN 0-13-629023-X

Symons, C.   Software Sizing and Estimating – Mk II Function Point Analysis, Wiley, 1991, ISBN 0-471-92985-9

Tudor, D.J and Tudor, I.J.   Systems Analysis and Design – A Comparison of Structured Methods, Macmillan Computer Science Series, 1997, ISBN 0-333-72139-X

Yourdon, E. and Constantine, L.   Structured Design, Yourdon Press, 1976, ISBN 0-917072-11-1

Yourdon, E.   Modern Structured Analysis, Prentice-Hall, 1989.

ISO 9001.   Quality Systems: Model for Quality Assurance in Design/Development, Production, Installation and Servicing, 1987

ISO 9000-3   Quality Management and Quality Assurance Standards, Part 3: Guidelines of ISO 9001 to the Development, Supply and Maintenance of Software, 1991

UK Government Publications

DTI and NCC   Starts Guide, Second Edition, 1987

HMSO   SSADM and GUI Design: A Project Manager's Guide, 1994, ISBN 0-11-330650-4

HMSO   Human Factors Guidelines for the Design of Computer-Based Systems, HUSAT Research Centre, 1988

CCTA, ISE Library   Improving the Maintainability of Software

CCTA, ISE Library   Estimating with MkII Function Point Analysis

Appendix C
Introducing DSDM into an Organisation: a Plan of Action

The introduction of DSDM into an organisation must be carefully planned and managed to achieve a successful outcome.

Firstly, the reasons for introducing DSDM must be understood. External pressures on the business may force the issue, such as market pressure or legislative changes. In these cases the business will be keen to apply DSDM to meet their needs, and will bring pressure to bear on their IT department. In other situations, IT departments themselves initiate the move towards DSDM, often because of the need to gain greater commitment and involvement from the business, in order to deliver the right systems.

In any situation, the business case for DSDM will need to be developed. It must show that there is a strong enough case for changing from the current approach to DSDM. It should be put together in close collaboration between the business and IT departments.

Once the case for introducing DSDM is established, it will be necessary to put together a plan for its implementation. The components of this plan are discussed below.

Identify a DSDM champion

The successful implementation of DSDM has often been driven by one individual who strongly believes in the method and is driven to challenge and change the existing organisation's culture and current practices wherever relevant. These champions will be invaluable in convincing the sceptics, especially if they occupy a senior position in the business.

Communicate the philosophy and concepts of DSDM to all concerned

This is normally by achieved by a series of DSDM Aware training courses, usually targeted to Senior Management and Board level (both business and IT), all affected categories of business users, and IT development and support staff. In larger organisations, these events are run for the group of people who will be involved on the first DSDM project and planned implementation.

Examine the current development practices and procedures, and compare with the DSDM approach

Many organisations find that they have already been using elements of DSDM, such as user involvement, empowerment, prototyping, facilitated workshops and timeboxing. By using examples of successful practices already in use, adopting DSDM can be seen to be building on existing best practice.

Using the same comparison, identify the areas that will need to be changed

In organisations where there is a large gap between the current culture and that required for DSDM, a full change management programme should be put together. This may require the use of specialist, external consultants. Even if the gap is relatively small, it is still necessary to put together a plan. Some typical issues that need addressing are empowerment, multi-skilled team members and technical skills. The use of the MoSCoW rules can help to prioritise the plan.

Where there are gaps in existing practices and procedures, the method of filling the gap must be identified either for action immediately, or during a pilot project which can feed its experiences back into the organisation's procedures. The latter approach should only be used for relatively minor changes to the current methods of working.

Gain support and commitment for all the activities in the plan

Once support is gained for the plan, it will be possible carry out the all necessary preparatory work in order to have a sound basis for starting on the first project.

Identify the first project

Use the DSDM Suitability Filter and Critical Success Factors to identify a suitable project. Some organisations will select projects to meet urgent business needs, where there is no alternative but DSDM to meet the tight deadline. Others will select a project for a business area, where they have already established good, close, working relationships with senior business management and key users. In all cases, assess the risks and agree how these will be managed.

A key concern will be selecting suitable team members using the DSDM role definitions for guidance.

Train the project team

All members of the team, both full and part time, should be trained using the appropriate accredited DSDM training courses. It may also be necessary to provide technical training for tools, configuration management, testing etc.

Set up the development environment

It is best to locate the DSDM team in a dedicated room, in the business department. This room should contain all the technical equipment required for the team.

Launch the project

Once everything is prepared, it is usual to have some type of project launch event. This may take the form of a presentation of the business vision by the Visionary, team building events, a social occasion, an open day or a combination of such events.

Run the first project

Often, an organisation will commission a DSDM Mentor to assist on the first project, to ensure that the DSDM approach is being followed correctly and that the team maintain their focus on delivering business benefits, throughout the project. Indeed a DSDM Mentor can be very useful before the project starts in helping to identify what changes to existing working practices should be considered.

Review the project

Following the successful implementation of the first project, it is recommended that some time is spent analysing the project, particularly to identify lessons learnt. What will be done differently the next time? What will be kept the same? Particular attention should be paid to documents, procedures and any conflicts with existing work practices. These results should be documented and fed into the next project.

Broadcast your success

It is useful to put together presentations, videos, newsletters, press articles, etc. to let everyone in the organisation know of the success. This often leads to other departments then asking for DSDM projects.

Submit for DSDM Practitioner examination

Members of the team may wish to apply for DSDM Practitioner certification, thus gaining a professional qualification in DSDM. Examination guidelines are available from the DSDM Consortium.

Prepare for the next DSDM projects

In the early stages of propagating DSDM in an organisation, many companies divide the existing DSDM team members into two new teams and supplement them with other inexperienced DSDM team members. This is seen as a way to grow more teams, whilst retaining some experienced DSDM developers in each team. Other organisations find splitting up successful teams too disruptive and keep successful teams together for as long as possible.

Finally, measure the business benefits

Were the anticipated benefits achieved? Has the business case put forward been substantiated? It is wise to consider both hard and soft benefits – one of the typical benefits of the first DSDM project is the clearer understanding in both business and IT of each other's different points of view. For some companies, this has considerably improved the relationship between business and IT departments.